Intercession

Intercession

A Theological and Practical Guide

Ormonde Plater

Cowley Publications

Lanham • Boulder • New York • Toronto • Plymouth, UK

Library of Congress Cataloging in Publication Data:
Plater, Ormonde
Intercession: a theological and practical guide / Ormonde Plater.
p.   cm.
Includes bibliographical references.
ISBN-10: 1-56101-115-0   ISBN-13: 978-1-56101-15-5 (alk. paper)
1. Intercessory prayer—Christianity 2. Intercessory Prayer—Episcopal Church.
1. Title.
BV210.2.P54   1995
264'.0301—dc20

95-19073

Scripture quotations and citations refer to the *New Revised Standard Version* of the Bible (NSRV), © 1989 by the Division of Christian Education of the National Council of the Churches of Christ in the United States of America.

Quotations from the *Supplemental Liturgical Materials 1991* are used by permission of the Church Hymnal Corporation, New York.

Cover detail: *Jesus and St. Peter's Mother-in-Law,* from the Hitda Codex, eleventh century, Cologne.

Cover design: Vicki Black

Printed in the United States of America

♾™ The paper used in this publication meets the minimum requirements of American National Standard for Information Sciences—Permanence of Paper for Printed Library Materials, ANSI/NISO Z39.48-1992.

A Cowley Publications Book
Published by Rowman & Littlefield Publishers, Inc.
4501 Forbes Boulevard, Suite 200, Lanham, Maryland 20706

Distributed by National Book Network

For the holy gathering of Saint Anna
in New Orleans.

Kyrie eleison.

Contents

Foreword xvii

Part I
Theology and History

1. A Song of Remembering . . . . **page 3**
Questions About Intercession 4
Several Theological Approaches 6
1. Sacrifice
2. Kingdom
3. Thanksgiving
4. Remembering

2. A Song of Speaking . . . . **page 12**
Ancient Origins 13
Jesus at Prayer 15
Apostolic Church 16

3. A Song of Offering . . . . **page 18**
Early Church 18
Eastern Orthodoxy 21
Middle Ages 21
Reformed Churches 22
Twentieth Century 23

6. Season by Season .... **page 54**

Advent 54

Christmas and Epiphany. 56
    The Weeks After the Epiphany

Lent 57
    Ash Wednesday
    The Sundays in Lent

Holy Week 59
    Palm Sunday
    Maundy Thursday
    Good Friday
    Holy Saturday

Easter 61
    The Great Vigil of Easter
    The Fifty Days of Easter
    Rogation Days
    Ascension Day
    The Day of Pentecost

The Season After Pentecost 63

7. Occasion by Occasion .... **page 65**

Feasts of Saints. 65

Catechumenate. 66

Baptism 66

Confirmation 67

Marriage. 68

Birth or Adoption of a Child 69

Ministry to the Sick 69

Death and Burial 69

Ordination 71

Celebration of a New Ministry 72

Consecration of a Church 72

Other Special Liturgies 73
    Dedication of Church Furnishings and Ornaments
    Founding of a Church
    Reaffirmation of Ordination Vows
    Welcoming New People to a Congregation
    When Members Leave a Congregation
    Celebration for a Home
    Various Blessings

8. Categories of Intercession. . . . . **page 77**
   1. The Church. 78
   2. The Nation and All in Authority 88
   3. The World 89
   4. The Community 92
   5. The Needy 93
   6. The Dead 99

9. Ancient Litanies . . . . **page 101**
   A. Prayers at the Eucharist 101
     Litany for the Catechumens
     Litany for the Energumens
     Litany for the Illuminands
     Litany for the Penitents
     Litany of the Faithful
   B. Prayers at the Daily Office 107
   C. Prayers at a Funeral 108

10. Sample Litanies . . . . **page 109**
   A. Prayers at Morning and Evening 109
     Morning
     Evening
   B. Prayers at the Eucharist 111
     A Litany for Rite One
     A Litany Based on Ancient Sources
     A Litany for Weekdays
   C. Prayers at Seasonal Liturgies 114
     Advent
     Christmas, Epiphany, and Baptism
     Lent (Sundays 1–3)
     Lent (Sundays 4–6)
     The Great Vigil of Easter
     The Fifty Days of Easter
   D. Prayers on Special Occasions 122
     Feasts of Saints
     Marriage
     Burial of the Dead

11. Music . . . . **page 126**
   Chants from the Past 127
   Kievan Chant 128
      Advent
      Christmas
      Lent
      Easter

12. A Guide for Study and Practice . . . . **page 132**
   Theological Background 132
      Chapter 1: A Song of Remembering
      Chapter 2: A Song of Speaking
      Chapter 3: A Song of Offering
      Chapter 4: Week by Week
      Chapter 5: Day by Day
      Chapter 6: Season by Season
   Composing the Prayers 135
      Sunday Intercessions
      Intercessions on Special Occasions
      Litanies
      Music

Foreword

A few days after finishing the first draft of this book, I had an unexpected chance to test on a large scale the ideas on intercession I have written about here. In late August of 1994, I attended the General Convention of the Episcopal Church as a member of the press. When I arrived at the convention hall, the liturgy coordinator asked me to compose the intercessions for the eucharist each morning. I proposed that I gather several persons for this purpose. Eventually Deacon Phina Borgeson and Sister Brenda Code, O.S.H., joined me.

Every afternoon we met and shared ideas, and one of us, in rotation, wrote six or seven simple, brief biddings for the next morning, using the forms in the prayer book as guides. There was an atmosphere of urgency in preparing the intercessions for each impending liturgy. We read the daily newspapers and looked at news programs on television. We listened carefully to the sometimes disturbed, sometimes uplifted mood of the large gathering. We wrote down prayer requests from slips of paper posted in the convention chapel. Somewhere between the minute details of individual lives and the grand issues of the church and the world, we tried to express needs, concerns, and hopes that touched the hearts of all, and to craft intercessions which all could hear and for which all could pray.

The experience convinces me that the intercessions of the Christian assembly need to be fresh and immediate. There is no great mystery or sophistication about writing intercessions and leading them. What we did for a gathering of thousands, the smallest congregation can do every Sunday. I hope that this book will take some of the mystery out of the process of preparing intercessions, and make intercessory prayer accessible for all who gather in the name of Christ.

This book is intended as a resource and help. It begins by laying a theological and historical basis for intercessory prayer. It then shows how intercession can be used in private prayer, in the daily prayer of the church, and in the eucharist and other rites of the Christian assembly. In this context I encourage the church to adapt and alter the printed prayer texts and to compose new litanies, as both the Episcopal Church and the Anglican Church of Canada allow.

In recent years many persons of talent have composed intercessions for the liturgies of Christian churches, and many writers have commented on intercessory prayer. As an Anglican writing primarily for Anglican readers in North America, in this book I am concerned chiefly with intercession in the *Book of Common Prayer* (1979) of the Episcopal Church and the *Book of Alternative Services* (1985) of the Anglican Church of Canada. I invite Anglicans in these two churches to share each other's forms of intercession and to learn from each other old and new ways of praying. Similarly, Anglicans can share texts and techniques with Christians in other traditions.

In addition to the main liturgical books used in the Anglican churches of North America, I refer to several collections of optional liturgies: *The Book of Occasional Services* (New York: Church Hymnal Corp., 1991); *Occasional Celebrations of the Anglican Church of Canada* (Toronto: Anglican Book Centre, 1992); and *Supplemental Liturgical Materials* (New York: Church Hymnal Corp., 1991). The following abbreviations will be used in references to these books:

Book of Common Prayer (1979)	BCP
Book of Alternative Services (1985)	BAS
Book of Occasional Services (1991)	BOS
Occasional Celebrations (1992)	OC
Supplemental Liturgical Materials (1991)	SLM

Page numbers referring to the last three books should be used with caution. The *Book of Occasional Services* (BOS) comes out in a new edition every few years, with one scheduled for early 1995. *Occasional Celebrations* (OC) is published in loose-leaf form "to facilitate ongoing expansion and change." Because there is a continuing need to develop new liturgical materials, *Supplemental Liturgical Materials* (SLM) will probably be revised or replaced.

Part I

❧

Theology and History

1

A Song of Remembering

At the lunch hour, an insurance salesman finds a storage room where he can be alone for a moment. He leans against a wall and thinks of his daughter, who is addicted to cocaine. He feels helpless and empty. In his weekly support group he has learned to pray for himself and others. Now he prays, "God, take her into your hands. Strengthen all of us who love her."

Scrubbing her hands as she prepares for surgery, a cardiologist mentally reviews the procedure. Then she pauses and tries to empty her mind of medical techniques. She thinks of the patient's name. "Lord, hear my prayer and help this sick man and the nurses and me."

An old woman looks at the television screen as the announcer speaks of civil war and thousands of refugees, many dying and dead, in an African nation. She searches in the back of the *Book of Common Prayer* and finds a collect about loving our enemies: "Deliver them and us from hatred, cruelty, and revenge; and in your good time enable us all to stand reconciled before you."

A man stands at the side of the hospital bed where his wife is dying of intestinal cancer. In the last few months they have learned to say evening prayer together. Now she is near death. As he holds her hand he prays from the prayer book. When he comes to the place for free intercession, he adds, "Father, bring her to a land of peace and grant her rest among your angels and saints."

A small group of parishioners meets every month to share stories about ministering to the sick in hospitals. When they finish they rise and form a circle with hands joined. In turn they pray for the people they have talked about. They present names to God. They ask God to help, be present, cure a disease, guide them in ministry. The last person says a brief, informal prayer.

It is Sunday morning. At the time for the prayers of the people, the deacon and three parishioners move to the lectern. A member of a prayer group reads the names of those celebrating birthdays and baptismal anniversaries during the coming week. A hospital minister announces the sick of the parish. The senior warden mentions several concerns of the community and adds, "I bid your prayers for this parish as we search for a new rector." The deacon asks if anyone else wants to speak. After several people have spoken, there is a period of silence. Then the deacon begins a litany by singing, "In peace, let us pray to the Lord."

Questions About Intercession

Even as Christians in many churches restore the vitality of intercessory prayer, they face questions about the meaning of prayer. What does it mean to ask God to have mercy on the sick and the suffering, travelers, prisoners, captives, the hungry and the homeless, the poor and the oppressed, the dying and the dead? Does God hear? Does God act? Does God even care?

At all times and in all places, Christians have asked God to intervene in human affairs, and they have relied on God to respond to their requests. The practice of seeking divine intervention implies a theology of intercession stemming from its ancient origins in the language of commerce. The God who sees and hears, who deals with human beings as one person to another (although as a superior to an inferior), is able and willing to set things right throughout creation. Answering our entreaties, God will bring peace into places of strife and discord, restore justice and mercy, heal the sick, and give the dead new life. All we have to do is ask, and whatever we ask, God will answer. God will respond with compassion and love, although not necessarily in a way or at a time that we expect.

The teaching of Jesus supports the biblical tradition embodied in our venerable practice:

> For everyone who asks receives, and everyone who searches finds, and for everyone who knocks, the door will be opened. (Matthew 7:8; Luke 11:10)

Passages such as this refer primarily to seeking and finding the gift of faith, but they also depict a world of defenseless creatures sheltered beneath the wings of God. All of us are on a journey to the kingdom of God. As that journey nears its end, God, responding to fervent prayer, will bring divine peace to all creation, from the newborn babe to the least significant atom.

While this concept of a personal God who intervenes in human lives remains traditional among Christian believers, it is no longer universally accepted. Especially in the western world, with its materialistic and scientific culture, some find it difficult to believe in a God whom one can debate, cajole, and even manipulate, or to rely on a God who places food in open mouths. The evidence throughout the world of unrelieved hunger, violence, poverty, death, oppression, and injustice suggests that the supreme being who breathed across the waters of chaos, forming the universe, has withdrawn and become remote and disinterested. For some, that God is dead.

Many of the difficulties with prayer today have their roots in ancient theologies. In the early church there were two opposite ways of looking at God: God completely down here, imminent and involved in the affairs of material beings, and God completely up there, transcendent and disengaged from all the creatures God had made. At their most extreme and heretical, on both ends, God disappears. The exclusively imminent God becomes swallowed up within creation; the exclusively transcendent God vanishes into infinity.

For orthodox Christians, God is both here and there, imminent and transcendent, visibly imprinted in created matter and invisibly exalted in distant majesty, an immutable Being deeply engaged with humanity and the history of the universe. This God of here and there comes among us, forms our lives, and informs our consciousness of divinity.

Belief in the Trinity and in Christ suggests a complex relationship between God and creation, in which unity and diversity live in delicate balance. When three persons coexist in one being, and human and divine natures in one person, we have within God a model of total engagement and total communion; each member (each person of God or nature of Christ) respects the integrity and individuality of the other. The God who took on human flesh cares profoundly about human beings, yet does not rearrange created matter every time it bends out of shape. The God who raised Christ from the dead offers eternal life to all creatures, yet does not meddle with human destiny every time human beings stray. Through the incarnation of Christ, God entered the material universe and human history. Through the resurrection of Christ, God overcame the limitations of sin and death. The language of love replaced the language of law and commerce.

More than twenty years ago the Episcopal Church attempted to address the difficulty of praying to a personal God who acts in the world. In preparing to revise the *Book of Common Prayer*, the Standing Liturgical Commission wrote that intercessory prayer has meaning on four levels:

(1) As an exercise in self-expression, by which we reveal our true feelings.

(2) As an exercise in illumination, by which we can see sickness, disorder, and other dire situations in the light of the cross and resurrection.

(3) As an exercise in commitment, by which we come to act for others.

(4) As access to God, by which prayer "commends the matter in hope and trust to the care of a merciful God."[1]

This list of meanings reflects much of the psychological and philosophical sentiments of the last two centuries. Concerned chiefly with the feelings and attitudes of those who pray, the list makes only a passing reference to a transcendent God who cares deeply about creation. Instead, it reveals a theological drift, thoroughly modern, in which God's healing action in the world has become vague and ambivalent. More important for our recovered understanding of the nature of the church, the list possesses little sense of prayer as an activity of gathered people who praise God in faith. Prayer has become an "exercise" like aerobics, designed to make one whole and hearty, performed in front of a spiritual video.

Several Theological Approaches

The ancient tradition of the church supports another interpretation of intercession. In this meaning, all prayer can be seen as part of an unending song to God our creator, sanctifier, and redeemer. This meaning comes from the liturgy of the Christian assembly, and it involves several theological approaches to intercession, including sacrifice, kingdom, thanksgiving, and remembering.

---

1   Standing Liturgical Commission of the Episcopal Church, *Prayers, Thanksgivings, and Litanies*, Prayer Book Studies 25 (New York: Church Hymnal Corp., 1973), 11-13.

1. Sacrifice

In this "absolutely essential act" of intercession we make the intercession of Christ our own.[2] We share in the royal priesthood of Christ, who intercedes continually for us in heaven. We perform a sacrificial act, part of a grand sequence of offerings that culminates in the eucharistic prayer and the feast of bread and wine.

The restoration of intercession to its position in the liturgy before the peace and eucharistic prayer makes this sequence clear. After we have heard the word of God and reflected on it, we offer prayers to God for all those in need. With uplifted hands we hold all these persons, all these concerns, and present them to God. In doing so, we also present ourselves. Ancient prayers of intercession ended with a commendation of "ourselves and one another to the living God through Christ."

Then we turn to each other and offer a sign of peace, forgiving each other for offenses and sealing us into one body. Because God is among us as we gather, and Christ is the body of those who gather, the offering of peace is a sacrifice in which we offer ourselves to God as a reconciled people.

Finally, when the table has been set and the meal prepared, we offer to God the bread and wine, those gifts that our hands have transformed into food and drink, and in so doing we again offer ourselves as a living sacrifice.

Many think of sacrifice as making a sizable donation or suffering a painful loss, often to the point of death, in order to benefit someone else or to advance a noble cause. This idea of sacrifice requires endurance through adversity. Americans during the Second World War sacrificed themselves for their country by enduring rationing and deprivation or by sending their sons into battle, perhaps to be wounded or killed. Giving money for the upkeep and programs of the church is sometimes regarded as a sacrifice, especially if the amount approaches a tithe.

In a common religious interpretation of sacrifice, one kills a victim and presents the body to a deity. Abraham placed his young son Isaac on an altar and prepared to kill him; at the last moment he killed and presented a ram to God, an acceptable substitute for Isaac. As an acceptable substitute for all humanity, Christ suffered and died on the cross, presenting himself to God. This idea of sacrifice requires the sacrificial victim to endure pain and often death.

---

2 Alexander Schmemann, *For the Life of the World: Sacraments and Orthodoxy* (Crestwood, N.Y.: St. Vladimir's Seminary Press, 1973), 44.

In another sense of the term, sacrifice means offering gifts to God. These gifts are not strange and wonderful novelties to God. God gives them to us, the fruits of creation, and then we fashion them with our hands and hold them up to God. Since God created all things, our offering of things acknowledges God's true ownership.

In the intercessions, the persons and concerns we offer to God—the danger and violence, the poverty and oppression, the sickness and death—are part of the human condition, utterly familiar to God. We offer them as a priestly people, awaiting the coming of the kingdom.

2. Kingdom

We are on a long journey, a crowd of people walking toward a mountain in the distance. As we reach the foothills and approach the mountain, it appears to come to meet us. Slowly it grows larger, emerging from the haze and becoming clearer, gaining color and shape and detail. Day by day our imagination swells to meet the mountain. We want to reach this goal above all else.

This is the highest mountain, "the mountain of the Lord's house" (Isaiah 2:2), where all peoples, nations, tribes, clans, and families will come together in peace, as they walk in the light of Christ. This is the kingdom of God. At sunrise and sunset on our journey, and at the evening meal, we pause and praise God and pray for ourselves, this gathered people on this journey. Then we pray for all those in danger and need. We are anticipating the kingdom.

With hope and confidence, we ask for healing in particular situations. Healing is for the journey. Some of us are unable to continue and fall by the wayside. We ask God to give sight to the blind, restore strength to the lame, give courage to the weak of heart, unite with us those who are estranged, so that they can rise, walk with the crowd, and see the mountain in the distance.

Healing is our joyful expectation as a people who pray, "your kingdom come," and who want Christ in his second coming to form the world in his image. Healing is a sign of the coming of the kingdom and a means of participating in the journey.

Advent gives Christians a rich opportunity to reflect on the kingdom, and to rejoice in the coming of God among us. Many of us think of Advent as a season of penitential preparation. Primarily it is a time of joyful expectation in which all creation is pregnant with the kingdom of God. In that season, and in the weeks leading up to it, we await with joy the second coming of Christ, revealed as a king in all his glory, and we pray for his coming.

Intercession is not an occasion for us to promote our own political or social program. We do not tell God what to do. It is not *our* kingdom that is coming, not *our* republic. Intercession is prayer for the reign of God. As we await the kingdom of God, we await the warm breath of God's love throughout creation.

3. Thanksgiving

In several places the prayer book allows us to use "intercessions and thanksgivings." We often think of these as two different but closely related types of prayer: intercession as asking for gifts and favors, thanksgiving as appreciation for receiving them. In the kingdom of God, however, past, present, and future escape the bounds of time. When we intercede, we are also thanking God for the topics of our prayer.

When we pray for the sake of others, our prayer draws its power from the creation of all things. This is revealed by the two accounts of creation in Genesis. In the first, more recent account, God creates the universe and the earth and all its inhabitants in six days. Twice God pauses to bless the living creatures of the water, the sky, and the land. Then God blesses the seventh day, sign of "all the work that he had done in creation" (Genesis 2:3). This list suggests a litany in which a leader recounts the mighty acts of God, and the people respond with shouts of glory, blessing, and thanksgiving.

The second, older account begins with a narrative about identity. Adam gives names to every living creature. To name a thing is to bless God for it. By naming God's creatures we bless them; by blessing them we call on God to protect them. Something similar happens when we intercede. To name living creatures in a prayer of intercession is to bless God for them, to give thanks for their creation, and to call on God for mercy, justice, peace, and forgiveness.

The use of blessing or naming in the creation narratives has influenced two later texts. The first is the late Hebrew song *Benedicite, omnia opera Domini*—now commonly know as "A Song of Creation"—in which the singers call on all creatures, animate and inanimate, to bless the Lord. The second is the thirteenth-century "Canticle of Brother Sun" by Francis of Assisi, expressing a similar theme. Both texts are lists in the form of litanies, in which the singers name one topic after another.

4. Remembering

All the various meanings of intercession come together in the activity of remembering. We tend to think of remembering as a mental excursion into the past: one "remembers" the Christmas of one's childhood. Its theological meaning, expressed by the Greek term *anamnesis*, refers to breaking out of the limitations of time and space.

Christians celebrate the eucharist because Christ commanded, "Do this for the remembrance *[anamnesis]* of me." By remembering the mighty acts of God in and through Christ, Christians experience the presence of Christ. Time and space vanish as we find Christ in our midst.

God remembers. In their liturgy the Russian Orthodox sing, "Remember your servants, Lord, when you come in your royal power." In the eucharistic prayer, after we have lifted hearts and voices, praising God for the mighty acts of creation and salvation, telling the story of Christ, and offering the holy gifts, we ask God to remember the church and various persons, and we pray for our inclusion with all who have gone before.

Remembering means not forgetting (*an-amnesia*); it makes us able to have a past. Having a past means having a present and a future, having a history. By remembering a past event, we take a journey into history. By remembering us, God gives us a past and a future, a history.

Remembering means putting things back together and making them whole. By sewing a severed limb back onto a body, reattaching its tissues and blood vessels and muscles, a surgeon re-members the body. Restoring a separated person back into the body of Christ, reattaching all its parts, God re-members the body. People, the church, the earth, all creatures are re-membered when God puts them back together. At the heart of its meaning, intercession is our song that God may put the church and all creation back together again.

ⓒ&

Why a *song* of remembering? All prayer is our song to God, sung with God and with all the creatures of God. With song we express our joy, find our way on our journey, and hold ourselves together as a community of Christ.

With song our prayer soars with the breath of God. Like the prophet Miriam and all the Israelite women with tambourines, like King David leaping with all his might, like Francis of Assisi clapping his hands and prancing, we dance before the Lord and sing our sacrifice of praise and thanksgiving.

With song our prayer follows a candle in the darkness. We may waver and wander away, but song brings us back to the path. Song guides the fallen and strengthens the fainthearted as we stumble along the way.

With song our prayer holds us together. Our voices seek the melody, and though we are many and different, we sing in unity of being. Singing as one choir as we move through the dark, we reflect the infinite harmony of the cosmos. Our voices are with the angels and all spiritual beings.

Sharing these qualities of song, intercession is our prayer to God to show mercy. As we pray to God for the benefit of others, we sing the song of remembering. As we sing the song of remembering, God re-members those who are many members.

Lord God, who makes the dawn and the dusk to sing for joy, hear us as we join our voices with your whole creation and grant that we may see the splendor of your love. Glory to you for ever.

2

A Song of Speaking

We understand intercession as prayer to God for the benefit of others. Christians pray for others in private and in the corporate liturgy of the church, especially its daily morning and evening prayer and its eucharist on Sundays and major feasts. Intercession is the sacred duty of all the baptized people of God, a priestly activity of high dignity for those in communion with God through Christ.

All prayer is conversation with God. Like other forms of prayer, intercession comes naturally to those who are accustomed to talking with a personal God. The God who resembles a strong, wise, and loving parent hears our requests and answers them. Like Jesus, we speak in familiar terms with our Father in heaven. We know that Jesus Christ is our true defender who will help us, the "one mediator between God and humankind" (1 Timothy 2:5). Within the family of God, prayer for the living and the dead, for individuals, things, and concerns, for the welfare of the gathered brothers and sisters, for all those in danger and need, and for all God's creation belongs to the normal discourse of Christian people.

As we consider intercession in the church today, it is important to look back to the origins of intercessory prayer in Christian scripture and tradition. Just as the theological implications of intercessory prayer today are shaped and informed by the theologies of those who have gone before us, so the forms and understandings of intercessory prayer we have today have their roots in earlier traditions of prayer and conversation with God recorded in scripture.

Ancient Origins

The origins of intercession lie deep in the cultic practices of ancient peoples. In the history of the Jewish people, they are recorded first in the story of Sodom. When Abraham hears that God intends to wipe out Sodom with all its people, he approaches God and asks:

> Will you indeed sweep away the righteous with the wicked? Suppose there are fifty righteous within the city; will you then sweep away the place and not forgive it for the fifty righteous who are in it? (Genesis 18:23-24)

God agrees to save Sodom if the city contains fifty righteous persons. By the time Abraham has finished bargaining, however, God has agreed to reduce number to ten. As it turns out, even that small number is too lofty for such a city, and God destroys Sodom.

Intercession thus begins with the language of the marketplace. Like camel traders or rug merchants, two parties state their requests, argue back and forth over quality and price, and strike a deal agreeable to both. Their speech is short, dignified, and humble, their bargaining shrewd, and even as they begin to haggle they perceive the possible result of the trade. Each knows that the other is exaggerating, one too high and one too low, and each is willing to adjust terms and to approach the other until they reach a point where trade is possible. They enjoy the competition and sharp humor of the exchange, for their dealing is not merely serious business but also recreation and social interchange.

In this trade, one party is superior to the other. God has goods to bestow that we can never match with goods of our own. The inequality of the merchants is not a barrier, however, to those who seek the infinite mercy of God. Though "dwelling in light inaccessible from before time and for ever" (as an ancient Christian prayer puts it), God is approachable by human beings on human terms. We can talk, we can argue, we can reason.

Ancient Israelites approached their human-like Yahweh as the only god with whom it was possible to have a reasonable transaction and make a fair trade. They came to Yahweh as members of a community, the people with whom Yahweh had made a binding covenant. They asked for all the blessings of this life, both corporate and individual: health, wealth, and happiness, many children and many cattle, fullness of life, and joy in their God.

Bargaining for life also takes place in the next great intercession of Israel, on Mount Sinai. When the people have melted their gold rings and cast them into the image of a calf, God threatens to consume them; their destruction would leave only Moses and his family to make a great nation. Moses reminds God of his promise to Abraham, Isaac, and Joseph:

> I will multiply your descendants like the stars of heaven, and all this land that I have promised I will give to your descendants, and they shall inherit it forever. (Exodus 32:13)

Faced by this reminder of earlier generosity, God changes his mind. The intercession of Moses for Israel holds an honest and trustworthy God to a bargain already made and sealed, however extravagant and undeserved by a fickle people.

Like Moses, the prophet Jeremiah seeks to intercede for Israel in peril. On this occasion of national apostasy, however, marked by the destruction of the temple, God's anger against the wickedness of the people is too great to turn aside. Three times God forbids Jeremiah to intercede:

> As for you, do not pray for this people, do not raise a cry or prayer on their behalf, and do not intercede with me, for I will not hear you. (Jeremiah 7:16; cf. 11:14, 14:11)

Jeremiah does not cry, God does not hear, and, without divine mercy, corruption continues to spread in the land.

Jewish tradition also credits Elijah the Tishbite with the role of intercessor. Centuries after the death of Elijah, the apostle James recalled:

> Elijah was a human being like us, and he prayed fervently that it might not rain, and for three years and six months it did not rain on the earth. Then he prayed again, and the heaven gave rain and the earth yielded its harvest. (James 5:17-18)

Although the source of this statement, found in 1 Kings 17-18, does not specifically mention intercessory prayer, Elijah's use of God's help in his confrontation with Ahab implies an abundance of intercession.

In another story of human need, on the other hand, Elijah's use of intercessory prayer is specifically present. During a long drought and famine, Elijah goes to live with a widow at Zarephath in Sidon. Eventually her son becomes ill and dies. Elijah prays to God to restore life to the son:

> O Lord my God, have you brought calamity even upon the widow with whom I am staying, by killing her son? (1 Kings 17:20)

God listens to Elijah's harangue and answers him favorably because her cause is doubly virtuous; the woman is a widow who has shown hospitality. In the Sidonian episode Elijah asks God to intervene in history by altering what is a disastrous course of events, bringing life out of death and rain out of drought. The story reveals intercessory prayer as part of the process of healing, the restoration to fullness of life in all creation.

From the exile until the time of Jesus, Jewish prayers tend to become more verbose and formal. The model for important discourse appears to have been the court of Solomon and subsequent kings, rather than the marketplace. When Nehemiah prays to "the great and awesome God" for the Jewish people (Nehemiah 1:5-11), his exalted language and obeisant attitude reflect his job as cupbearer to the Persian king. In post-exilic prayers, God sits on the level of an infinitely higher superior, an oriental potentate who metes out justice and mercy to many inferior supplicants.

Jesus at Prayer

Reverting to the earlier style of prayer, Jesus addresses God directly and simply. God still occupies the palace throne, but he deals with supplicants like a king visiting the marketplace. The tone of the discourse also suggests a son addressing the patriarch of a clan with respect, honor, and love.

"Father, I thank you for having heard me," Jesus says just before he calls Lazarus to come out of the tomb (John 11:41). Apparently, Lazarus has already risen from the dead, the beneficiary of Jesus' prayer to his Father. Similarly, the long high-priestly prayer in John's gospel suggests modest, direct intercession for the followers of Jesus:

> Holy Father, protect them in your name that you have given me, so that they may be one, as we are one. (John 17:11)

Jesus teaches his disciples that their intercession depends upon their remaining in the body of the faithful:

> If you abide in me, and my words abide in you, ask for whatever you wish, and it will be done for you. (John 15:7)

By the time of the composition of this gospel, the community for whom John wrote had become an unmanageable group living in a hostile world.

Jesus prays with confidence to his Father, and he assures us that God hears our prayers also. After he has taught his disciples to pray with what we now know as the Lord's Prayer, he tells them that God will give persistent entreaters whatever they need:

Ask, and it will be given you; search, and you will find; knock, and the door will be opened for you. For everyone who asks receives, and everyone who searches finds, and for everyone who knocks, the door will be opened. (Luke 11:9-10)

The prayer of Jesus to his Father is important for our understanding of intercession. God will hear our prayer because Jesus prays with the same breath as ours. Jesus inherits the mantle of the *'ebed Yahweh*, the Servant of the Lord, who "bore the sin of many, and made intercession for the transgressors" (Isaiah 53:12). Jesus is the supreme intercessor, the eternal high priest who "is able for all time to save those who approach God through him, since he always lives to make intercession for them" (Hebrews 7:25).

Apostolic Church

In the decades after the resurrection of Jesus, the apostolic churches prayed mainly for themselves and each other. Their intercessory prayer included the old themes of health, wealth, and fullness of life. In his letter to the Romans, Paul prays for a safe journey to Rome (1:10) and for the salvation of the Jews (10:1); he asks the Romans to join him in praying for his deliverance from the unbelievers in Judea and for his ministry in Jerusalem (15:31). The author of the letter to the Ephesians prays for spiritual strength for his audience (3:16). He asks them to "persevere in supplication for all the saints" and to pray also for his bold proclamation of the gospel (6:18-20). James emphasizes the connection between intercession and healing:

Are any among you sick? They should call for the elders of the church and have them pray over them, anointing them with oil in the name of the Lord. (James 5:14)

God will answer, saving the sick and raising them up, but the main response will be spiritual, the forgiveness of sins.

The fullest authorization for intercessory prayer in the New Testament can be found in 1 Timothy, at the head of a long list of instructions about church order:

> First of all, then, I urge that supplications, prayers, intercessions, and thanksgivings be made for everyone, for kings and all who are in high positions, so that we may lead a quiet and peaceable life in all godliness and dignity. This is right and is acceptable in the sight of God our Savior, who desires everyone to be saved and to come to the knowledge of the truth. For there is one God; there is also one mediator between God and humankind, Christ Jesus, himself human, who gave himself a ransom for all—this was attested at the right time. (1 Timothy 2:1-6)

In this passage, "supplications, prayers, intercessions, and thanksgivings" are not four separate kinds of prayer but four ways of describing prayer, perhaps with subtle distinctions.

In his letters Paul always combines praise and thanksgiving with petitions for himself and other persons, and the writer to Timothy follows Paul's custom. As in the high-priestly prayer in John, the passage from the letter to Timothy emphasizes entreaties for the sake of the Christian community. Although the prime beneficiaries of the suggested prayer are those in political authority, the real purpose is to support the young church. With the help of God, Christians formerly persecuted by bad rulers will now enjoy the peace and freedom to be good citizens of Rome.

ᶜᴿ

As we have seen, each place and age has its own style of speaking, and this includes the language of prayer. In its earliest known form, intercessory prayer reflected the plain language of trade and commerce, and although later Jewish prayers became elegant and flowery, Jesus returned to the simple, direct style of his ancient ancestors. This return was appropriate, for Jesus addressed God in love, as his Father with whom he shares the closest intimacy of being. Whether near at hand or far away, in the marketplace or on the throne, God through Jesus enters into speech with us, hears our requests, and answers them. Our speaking with God thus rises to the level of song.

3

A Song of Offering

The history of Christian intercession after the time of the apostolic church reveals a complicated evolution. After developing in the early church as a vital part of the eucharistic liturgy and daily prayer, intercessory prayer gradually shrank from public view during the middle ages. Its modern revival dates from the Reformation, but only during recent decades have the public intercessions been restored to the people as prayers not just of the ordained but of all the faithful.

Early Church

In the church of the first and second centuries, intercession became a prominent part of the eucharist and of the daily prayer of the community.[1] This is evident in the earliest surviving eucharistic prayer, contained in the *Didache*, a document of the late first or early second century. The prayer ends with an intercessory petition linking the holy bread with the holy people:

> As this broken bread was scattered on the mountains, yet was gathered and made one, so gather your church from the ends of the earth into your kingdom. For yours is the glory and the power through Jesus Christ for ever and ever.

---

1 For another account of intercession from the early church to the present, see David Enderton Johnson, *The Prayers of the People: Ways to Make Them Your Own* (Cincinnati: Forward Movement Publications, 1988), 1-6.

Another text of the time locates intercessions in their customary place as prayers of the faithful. In his *First Apology*, written about the year 150, Justin Martyr described the freshly baptized Christian as one who immediately joins an assembly where the people "offer prayers for ourselves, for the person who has been illuminated, and for others throughout the world, with great earnestness." Presumably these prayers (like eucharistic prayers in the early church) were free compositions based on a standard pattern.

Although we do not have any idea what form the earliest intercessions took, later evidence suggests that they were biddings announced by a leader (perhaps a deacon), to which the people responded with silence or with a sung refrain, such as *Kyrie eleison*. Following the intercessions, the people exchanged the kiss of peace and the president (the bishop) offered the thanksgiving over bread and wine. In his *Apostolic Tradition* (c. 215), Hippolytus affirms this sequence and its meaning:

> Then [after the water baptism and anointing] they shall pray with all the people.
> But they shall not previously pray with the faithful until they have undergone
> all these things.

Thus, the first priestly act of a new Christian was to join the assembly in the prayers of the faithful.

One critical liturgical issue in the early church concerned the Trinity. To which person was the assembly praying? Usually, if not always, it was God the Father, whom one approached through God the Son. Early in the third century, Origen, a teacher in the catechetical school in Alexandria, wrote that Christians should address intercession "or supplicatory prayer" not to Christ but "to the God of the whole universe, the Father, to whom also our Savior prayed" (*De Oratione*). Origen's opinion probably reflected the common liturgical practice of the day, which included Alexandria and the other churches of the East and Rome.

Our most detailed evidence of intercession in the liturgy comes from the late fourth century. The *Apostolic Constitutions*, written in Antioch about the year 380, shows that Syrian Christians were making extensive use of intercessory prayer. Following the homily in the eucharist, five litanies of varying length were offered. The first four were for the benefit of special groups of worshipers: catechumens (those preparing for baptism), energumens (those possessed by evil spirits), illuminands (those about to be baptized), and penitents (those undergoing public penance). A deacon led each litany while the people made their responses; then the bishop prayed at length, and the deacon told the group to leave.

After the preliminary litanies, a deacon called on those who remained (the faithful) to begin the general intercessions:

All we the faithful,
  let us bend the knee,
let us pray to God through Christ,
  let us all fervently call upon God through Christ.

The biddings that followed, each beginning with "For" and sometimes including "that" clauses, covered peace in the world and in the churches, bishops, presbyters, deacons, readers, singers, virgins, widows, orphans, married women, pregnant women, ascetics, those who do good works and give alms to the needy, the newly baptized, the sick, travelers by water or land, those in mines, in exile, in prison, or in bonds, enemies of the faithful, the unconverted, "the children of the church," one another, and every Christian. As in the earlier litanies, after each bidding the people responded with a cry, such as *Kyrie eleison*. The bishop's prayer led to the kiss of peace and the preparation of the gifts. The eucharistic prayer, which the bishop prayed just before the closing doxology, also contained many intercessions.

The morning and evening offices of the ancient Syrian church also contained litanies of intercession. Because these liturgies were sung in the bishop's church, or cathedral, they are commonly called "cathedral" offices. At sunset the deacon led an extensive litany, which ended with biddings for the coming night, an angel of peace, things good and profitable to souls, a Christian death, freedom from sin, and a life without reproach. Morning intercessions were similar. As in the eucharist, both litanies ended with the instruction: "Let us commend ourselves and one another to the living God through Christ."

The daily offices also contained litanies for catechumens, energumens, illuminands, and penitents. Similarly, burial of the dead, when the faithful gathered in a cemetery to celebrate the eucharist, included a litany for the repose of the dead person and for all "who are at rest in Christ."[2]

---

2 The litanies in the *Apostolic Constitutions* are reprinted in chapter 9 of this book, starting on page 101.

Eastern Orthodoxy

In the Eastern Orthodox litany of later centuries, used to this day, a subtle thematic change can be seen from the litanies of the early Syrian church. The "Lord" to whom the Orthodox Christian prays is Christ, and thus the litany ends: "Let us commend ourselves and one another and all our lives to Christ." Nicholas Cabasilas, a Byzantine theologian of the fourteenth century who wrote a famous commentary on the Divine Liturgy, observed that in the opening litany "the faithful ask for one thing only—mercy." This cry of *Kyrie eleison* (Lord, have mercy) "implies both gratitude and confession" and is a request for the kingdom of God.

Why do Orthodox worshipers request the kingdom so often and in so many places? By the eighth century, the number of Byzantine litanies had greatly increased, and their subject matter had expanded. The litany originally found at the close of the liturgy of the word (the readings and homily) had become distributed in several places. The Liturgy of Saint John Chrysostom, widely used in Eastern Orthodox churches, contains nine *ektenias* or litanies: at the beginning (the Great *Ektene* or Litany of Peace); after the first two antiphons (the Little *Ektenias*); after the gospel and sermon (the Fervent Litany); at the dismissal of the catechumens; after that dismissal (the Prayers of the Faithful); before the anaphora (the eucharistic prayer); and before and after communion. Some of these litanies, especially the first, are long and comprehensive; most are brief. Taken together, the diaconal litanies and the intercessions of the anaphora covered all the dangers and needs, spiritual and material, of the church and the world.

Scholars have put forth several reasons for this expansion of intercessory material into multiple places: the litanies filled silences, they occupied the attention of easily distracted worshipers, they are fragments of earlier prayer services. Most likely, they addressed the spiritual needs of eastern Christians, whose appetite for worship often required intense and repetitive prayer. These litanies were concrete, brief, and vivid. They dealt with ordinary human concerns, and they covered them thoroughly.

Middle Ages

In the West a different transformation took place, by which public intercession virtually disappeared from the mass. Early liturgies in Rome, Gaul, and Spain had prayers of the faithful in the ancient position, at the end of the liturgy of the word. These primitive Roman prayers survive in the solemn form still used by many Anglicans on Good Friday, a long series of biddings sung by a deacon, each followed by silence and a collect sung by the presider. After each bidding the deacon intoned, *Flectamus genua* (Let us bend the knee) and, after a while, *Levate* (Arise); these intervals allowed the people to pray silently.

By the eighth century, when the Roman rite began to replace almost all the other western rites, the solemn intercessions had vanished as a coherent unit. Scraps of intercessory material appeared in scattered places. Repeated chants of *Kyrie eleison* and *Christe eleison* occurred within the entrance rite, and a single *oremus* (let us pray) remained stranded at the start of the offertory.

Intercession—primarily for members of the church, living and dead, with commemoration of the saints—formed a large part of the eucharistic prayer, the canon of the mass. Since the priest said the canon silently, the people could neither hear the intercessions nor pray them. This displacement accompanied a shift in theology and piety, by which the priest became the primary minister of the mass. The people (if any were present) watched and prayed in silence during an unintelligible and often unspoken liturgy.

When the popular cathedral offices began to die out in the West, they gave way almost entirely to monastic offices, which were more meditative in character and prayed by those in monastic orders. In these liturgies the intercessions of the daily office were reduced to a series of verses taken from the psalms. Since the offices were sung in Latin, most Christians could not understand them.

Deprived of verbal expression in the formal liturgy, medieval Christians resorted to private prayer for intercession. It became common to invoke the saints. In a mild form of invocation, the greeting *Ave Maria* ends: "Holy Mary, Mother of God, pray for us sinners now and at the hour of our death." This simply acknowledges that we the living are in communion with the dead and can ask them to pray for us. In more extreme forms, the saints became mediators for Christ, or doorkeepers providing access to him. Much of medieval piety focused on the Virgin Mary, whose closeness to her son guaranteed that he would listen to her before all others. Mary therefore assumed the role of chief intercessor and even mediatrix with God.

Reformed Churches

The reformers of the sixteenth century were concerned with restoring Christian worship to its roots in scripture. In the 1549 *Book of Common Prayer*, Thomas Cranmer regrouped the intercessions of the Sarum mass as a prayer "for the whole state of Christ's Church" and placed them immediately after the *Sanctus*. This long prayer continued the medieval tradition of intercessions within the canon of the mass. While carefully avoiding any hint of invocation, Cranmer's prayer closed with a strong affirmation of the communion of saints. Its final paragraph included prayer for the dead and praise for "the glorious and most blessed Virgin Mary" and other saints. Since the priest or deacon sang or said these intercessions in the vernacular, the people could at least hear and understand them.

In the 1552 prayer book, Cranmer moved the prayer of intercession to the "Gallican position" (after the practice of the ancient church in Gaul), just before the confession of sin, which preceded the eucharistic prayer. (There was no offering of gifts.) He also removed prayer for the dead and praise for Mary and the saints, and thus the intercessions became limited to the church militant here on earth. The priest said the prayer, and at the end the people (or parish clerk) responded "Amen." At this time, as in the middle ages, the people were present mainly as passive observers; if they were literate they could read along in their prayer books. The 1552 form of intercession and its Gallican position before the confession remained standard in Anglican liturgies until the twentieth century.

In his design for worship on Sunday morning Cranmer envisioned a three-part sequence: matins, litany, and communion. Much of the intercessory material omitted from the communion service appeared in the second of these parts. At considerable length and embracing many needs and concerns, the Great Litany of 1544 recalls the intercessions of the ancient Syrian church. During the eighteenth and nineteenth centuries, however, Anglican worship in most places lost the three-part sequence, as the typical Sunday service (morning or evening) became the daily office, and the Great Litany became as rare as Holy Communion. However, this loss was public only, and Christians continued to pray privately for others. In all ages, in East and West, the desperate need for intercession is universal and transcends liturgical trends.

Twentieth Century

The 1928 *Book of Common Prayer* of the Episcopal Church followed the pattern of Anglican worship that evolved during the Reformation. Intercessions took the form of prayers by the presiding priest, to which the people replied "Amen." Those attending morning prayer (the most common service at the main liturgy in most places) heard the priest read several collects after the Lord's Prayer, including one for the President and all in civil authority, one for the clergy and people, and one for "all sorts and conditions of men," especially "all those who are in any ways afflicted, or distressed, in mind, body, or estate." At this point the priest would insert names. There was no provision for prayer for the dead. Then, since there was no eucharistic prayer or communion, the congregation and priest said the General Thanksgiving. Evening prayer had a similar conclusion.

When Holy Communion was celebrated, after the offertory the priest often asked the people to intercede secretly; sometimes he read a list of names for the "special intentions" of the eucharist. Then he said a long prayer "for the whole state of Christ's Church." This concluded with a petition to God for the dead, "beseeching thee to grant them continual growth in thy love and service." At the end of the prayer the people responded "Amen." Toward the end of the eucharistic prayer the priest read supplications for the communicants and "all thy whole Church."

For many Episcopalians and other Anglicans, these provisions for intercessory prayer seemed aloof and insufficient. A large body of private prayers, including forms for intercession, has come into existence during the last two centuries. Both Anglo-Catholics and Evangelicals have been at the forefront of this renewed use of intercessory prayer: for example, the still-popular *Saint Augustine's Prayer Book*[3] contains intercessory prayers, devotions, and litanies, including many prayers for the sick, the dying, and the dead.

Starting in the 1960s, many churches of the West began to provide for stronger and more comprehensive intercession in the eucharist. Interest in intercession is especially evident in the *Book of Common Prayer* of the Episcopal Church (1979) and the *Book of Alternative Services* in Canada (1985), and intercession continues to be a concern in the optional and supplementary liturgies of these churches.

In the design of the revised prayer books, the intercessory prayers of the people (the faithful) occur in the ancient position, at the end of the liturgy of the word. These prayers reveal a shift away from petitions confined almost exclusively to the church, its clergy and people, and include petitions for the world, the nation, and all rulers (Christian or not), for the concerns of the local citizenry, and for the needs of all persons. Now the dead for whom Christians pray are not merely the "faithful" departed; they include all the dead whom we wish to commend to the hand of God.

These changes came from a sincere effort by modern revisers to reform worship following ancient models. Their motive was not antiquarian, but

---

3   West Park, N.Y.: Holy Cross Publications, 1967.

theological and practical, as our understanding of God has again focused on a God who is more personal and involved in human lives. Also lying behind the revival of intercessory prayer in the late twentieth century are the social, political, and military upheavals of the last two centuries. Scientific and industrial revolutions have left behind them the scarred landscape of the modern wasteland, with its human disruptions and ecological disasters. Warfare has reaped millions of wounded and dead. For many people living in this world of present and promised cataclysm, intercessory prayer has become an imperative, the cry for God's mercy an absolute necessity.

☙

How shall we sing the Lord's song upon an alien soil? In the liturgical sequence described by Justin Martyr in the second century, Christians make three offerings in the liturgy: prayers for the whole world, the kiss of peace, and gifts of bread and wine. Each offering prepares for and leads into the next one. Intercession makes possible the peace, and peace makes possible the bread and wine. Each action of the liturgy prepares for what is to follow, making us ready and able to lift our hearts and give thanks and receive the body and blood of Christ, at last uniting us in full communion with God and each other.

Part II

❧

Practical Guides to Intercession

4

Week by Week

Because Anglicans are accustomed to praying with a book, when we intercede in the Sunday eucharist we typically use the printed forms contained in the prayer book. It may come as a surprise to some that we are not *required* to use them. Many Episcopal congregations use only the texts in the *Book of Common Prayer* for their prayers of the people, but the church intends these forms mainly as models, guides, and inspirations. They show us *how* to intercede.

The prayer book encourages us to adapt these forms and to create new ones; by using the general models of intercession in the prayer book, we are able to compose our own local and indigenous forms. Marion J. Hatchett observes, "Adaptations or insertions suited to the occasion may be made in any of these [prayer book forms], and there is freedom to devise other forms."[1] This principle is expressed even more forcefully in the *Supplemental Liturgical Materials* of the Episcopal Church:

> Of the six forms provided [in the *Book of Common Prayer*], none are required. Any of them may be used or adapted to the occasion. They may also be replaced

---

1 Marion J. Hatchett, *Commentary on the American Prayer Book* (New York: The Seabury Press, 1980), 336. For another commentary on the American and Canadian intercessions, see David Enderton Johnson, *The Prayers of the People: Ways to Make Them Your Own* (Cincinnati: Forward Movement Publications, 1988), 20-41. Johnson also reproduces the litanies of the Anglican Church of Canada, 42-60.

by other forms. All that is required is that the topics listed at the top of page 383 be included in the prayers. (SLM 33)

Similar freedom exists in the Canadian *Book of Alternative Services*:

Thanksgiving and intercessions may take an extempore form following the headings given [for the prayers of the people], or one of the forms provided may be used. (BAS 176)

Thus, in the Anglican liturgies of the United States and Canada, the opportunity to change, compose, and even freely offer intercessory prayer is a gift to the eucharistic community. Our churches invite us to use our sensitivity and imagination in the most creative part of the liturgy.

Indigenous forms of intercession are desirable and sensible. They express the character of the community that prays them, and they enable that assembly to respond quickly to the changing needs, hopes, and concerns of the church and the world.

The process of learning to compose and lead intercessions in the eucharist begins with becoming familiar with the printed forms of general intercession in the prayer book. These forms are exercises in the history and structure of intercessory prayer.

A. Models of Intercession

The *Book of Common Prayer*
Rite One

In Rite One of the Holy Eucharist in the Episcopal Church we may use either the familiar prayer, as printed, or any other form of intercession. The prayer book directs us to offer intercessions "according to the following prayer, or in accordance with the directions on page 383." The "following prayer" is the prayer "for the whole state of Christ's Church and the world" (BCP 328, see BAS 235) discussed here.[2]

The present prayer "for the whole state of Christ's church" in Rite One and the Canadian 1962 eucharist retains the structure, content, and language of Anglican intercessions from 1549 until the 1960s. The ancestry of this prayer goes back

---

2   For "the directions on page 383" see the list of six topics discussed later in this chapter under Rite Two. These topics are: the church, the nation and all in authority, the world, the local community, those who suffer and those in trouble, and the dead.

to the medieval mass in Latin. In the old Roman canon of the mass, after the *Sanctus*, or while the choir sang an extended *Sanctus*, the priest silently prayed for the living—a series of petitions covering the church, the clergy, those who offered gifts, and all those present. Toward the end of the canon he silently prayed for the dead. These petitions for the living and the dead were linked with commemorations of the blessed Virgin Mary and other saints.

In the 1549 prayer book, Cranmer revised all these petitions, strung them together as one prayer in much the same order, and inserted them after the *Sanctus*. The rubrics directed the priest to "saye or syng, playnly and distinctly," both the intercessions and the "prayer of consecration" that followed.

In the second prayer book of 1552, Cranmer deleted prayer for the dead and commemoration of saints. He moved the intercessions to a place before the general confession and eucharistic prayer, as a separate prayer said by the priest. With minor changes in 1662 and later (including prayer for the dead in the American 1928 prayer book), the 1552 prayer remained the Anglican standard for four centuries.

The revisions of recent years in the Anglican communion have restored the general intercessions to their ancient place between the sermon (and Nicene Creed) and the kiss of peace. In the 1979 prayer book deacons and other baptized persons were designated to lead the prayer, and the people were allowed to make a response after each petition (although no text was suggested). The 1962 eucharistic liturgy of Canada allows the use of "all or portions" of the prayer or of a litany printed after it (BAS 235).

The form of the present prayer reflects its origins as a series of petitions addressed by the priest to God, and, despite the permission for responses, in many places it remains a long, formal monologue. However, the rubrics allow us to change the prayer or to use another form, and now that deacons and other persons may lead the prayer, it may be appropriate to recast the monologue in litany form—perhaps using Form I or Form IV as guides—or to replace it entirely.[3]

Rite Two

In Rite Two of the Holy Eucharist, at the place for the prayers of the people after the sermon and the Nicene Creed, the Episcopal prayer book directs us to offer intercessory prayer for:

---

3 For a litany version of this prayer, see page 111.

- The Universal Church, its members, and its mission;
- The Nation and all in authority;
- The welfare of the world;
- The concerns of the local community;
- Those who suffer and those in any trouble;
- The departed (with commemoration of a saint when appropriate). (BCP 359)

For examples of suitable intercessions, the directions point us to page 383 of the *Book of Common Prayer*. The Canadian church has a similar rubric (BAS 190).

The directions on page 383 repeat the six categories of subject matter and print six forms of intercessions that "may be used." The prayer book adds: "Adaptations or insertions suitable to the occasion may be used." The language "may be conformed" to Rite One or Rite Two, whichever is being used. The presider "may introduce" the intercessions with a sentence inviting the people to pray.[4]

The governing word in all these directions is *may*. If a congregation uses the six categories, it *may* intercede in several ways. The six forms show suitable ways of going about the task of intercession. Although these are the main ways, there are also other ways. The congregation decides whether it uses only the printed forms—one or two, or several, or all six in rotation—or adapts and composes intercessions. The congregation's needs, age, demography, social composition, and gifts of creativity all help to shape the prayer of the assembly. The prayer of a large cathedral may differ greatly from that of a small, inner-city congregation, the prayer of a seminary from that of a suburban parish. In one there may be formality, in another informality, in one a sense of history and tradition, in another a sense of immediacy and locality.

Form I (BCP 383)

This litany follows the structure and style of classic litanies in Eastern Orthodox liturgies from the fourth century to this day. Included are most of the biddings in the Great *Ektene*, with a few biddings from other litanies. The form also addresses modern concerns, as in a bidding for "the good earth" and a phrase concerning "the unemployed and the destitute." Ancient travelers went by land

---

4   These directions and six forms of intercession were first published by the Episcopal Church in 1970, as part of proposals for trial use. See *The Holy Eucharist*, Prayer Book Studies 21 (New York: Church Hymnal Corp., 1970), 111-128. There were originally seven forms; one of them, the solemn collects, was later moved to the liturgy of Good Friday. With only a few minor changes, the proposals were incorporated intact in the 1979 prayer book.

or water; to these have been added air and even outer space. The litany includes a bidding for "the absolution and remission of our sins and offenses," for use mainly when the liturgy does not include a formal confession of sins.

Along with Form V (also based on classic models), Form I is especially suitable for Sundays and major feasts. It uses a deacon or other leader, who directs the people in a long series of biddings. It provides for interaction between the leader and the people, and it is designed for chanting, or at least a sung response by the people.[5]

Supplemental Liturgical Materials claims that Forms I and V address the second person of the Trinity (SLM 33). The historical evidence is ambiguous, however, and the text is unclear. Only the last bidding points to Christ, and most collects that summarize and conclude such litanies address the first person of the Trinity.

The Canadian version of this form appears in two places: Litany 1 (BAS 110) and the alternative litany for the 1962 eucharist (BAS 236).

Form II (BCP 385)

This is a modern composition by a priest of the Episcopal Church in the 1960s, with roots in the ancient litanies, since it is a series of biddings addressed to the people, followed by silences. No response is provided, but worshipers may take advantage of the rubric to "offer their own prayers, either silently or aloud," during periods of silence, or to make their own biddings.

The open structure is especially suitable for small assemblies or for groups accustomed to expanding the formal intercessions with their own names and concerns. The Canadian version of this form, Litany 17, provides a collect after each bidding (BAS 123).

Form III (BCP 387)

This form comes from the 1966 experimental liturgy of Anglicans in New Zealand, which has since been replaced by indigenous liturgies containing several different forms. The structure resembles the suffrages in the daily office, a dialogue with God. The form thus reflects our Anglican heritage in which, until about a generation ago, morning prayer was the most common service on Sunday morning. A leader states the subject of each intention (God, do such and such), and the congregation responds with the intention ("That...") or, in the last two petitions, completes the statement. Each response is different from the one before.

---

5 For another version of the Orthodox litany, see page 112.

Although Form III is popular at daily celebrations because of its brevity, it is not suitable for most Sunday and festal eucharists. A variable dialogue is difficult to sing, and unless the people have memorized the text through frequent use, they must read from the prayer book during the intercessions.

There is no Canadian version of this form.

Form IV (BCP 388)

This form is a version of the 1967 Second Series experimental liturgy of the Church of England, twice revised; it was slightly changed for the 1979 prayer book. The form suggests the prayer "for the whole state of Christ's church," with petitions in the style of collect clauses. Silence follows each petition, after which the deacon or other leader says or sings, "Lord, in your mercy," and the people respond, "Hear our prayer."

The formal language and structure of Form IV make it suitable for use on Sundays and feasts, especially when the eucharist is Rite One. It may also be changed into a litany addressed to the people, with the same concluding versicle but with biddings that begin "For" or "That."

There is no Canadian version of this form.

Form V (BCP 389)

The original litany was composed in 1965 as the *oración de los fieles* in a Spanish-language mass. As an adaptation of Eastern Orthodox litanies, it was intended for only the most solemn days. With the same elegant style and long biddings of the Spanish-language litany, the present litany is also appropriate for Sundays and feasts.

The structure of most of the biddings is "For..., that..."; the litany closes with a commemoration of Mary and the saints. One permissible bidding asks for "the forgiveness of our sins," and another is an open form, allowing for special needs and concerns.

The rubrics suggest either a concluding collect or a doxology. Instead of the brief doxology printed in the text, a better choice would be Collect 5 (BCP 395), which is a more accurate rendering of the Eastern Orthodox original.

There is no Canadian version of this form.

Form VI (BCP 392)

This form is a compilation from several sources in the Episcopal Church, especially a litany authorized by the Special General Convention II in 1969 for use with the

1967 *Liturgy of the Lord's Supper*. In 1970 these were rearranged for the present form.

During the first half of the litany the leader and people pray responsively, each phrase beginning with the word "For." The second half consists of three periods of silence, in which the people add special needs and concerns, thanksgivings, and names of the dead; a versicle from scripture follows each silence. The litany may end with a general confession of sin. The presider concludes with either an absolution or a collect; if the confession is used, an absolution is not necessary.

Form VI tries to accomplish a multitude of liturgical tasks in a multitude of ways. It uses three types of prayer, moving from intercession to thanksgiving to confession. This mixture may prove confusing, since the main purpose of the general intercessions is to pray for the needs of others. The form also mixes styles, combining "for" petitions, versicles, and free prayer. Like Form III, the people must have the text in front of them if they have not memorized the responses.

The Canadian version of this form is Litany 18 (BAS 126).

Other Models of Intercession
Anglican Church of Canada

The 1985 *Book of Alternative Services* of the Anglican Church of Canada provides eighteen litanies for the daily office and eucharist (BAS 110-127). The book intends them only as models of intercessory prayer:

> They ought not to become the standard forms used in a parish, but should be
> adapted with imagination to meet the needs of the local Church. (BAS 177)

The eucharist and both offices contain directions similar to those in the American prayer book, calling on the community to intercede in six categories.

The first Canadian litany, like the American Form I, is a modern version of the Great Litany in Eastern Orthodox liturgies. It uses biddings beginning with "For" and ending with "let us pray to the Lord."

The rest of the litanies are diverse in form, style, and purpose. Some begin with "That," "We pray," and "Let us pray for." Some address the people, some God. Litanies 2-8 are for general use. There are litanies for morning (9), evening (10), and late evening (11); for the seasons of Advent (12, in which each petition is an O Antiphon), Incarnation (13, in which each petition starts with "By the..."), Lent (14, "For..."), and Easter (15, "That..."); and for the Holy Spirit (16, "Come, Holy Spirit..."). Litany 17 (expanded from Form IV) consists of biddings and collects like the old Roman intercessions now used on Good Friday, and Litany 18 (similar to Form VI) is responsive.

Some Episcopal congregations use the Canadian book as a resource for their own intercessions. They use the litanies intact with minor changes, or they adapt them freely.

Roman Catholic Church

In the Roman Catholic Church in the United States, several volumes have been published containing intercessions for Sundays, solemnities, other feasts, and votive and ritual masses. A typical text is *The Prayer of the Faithful for the Sundays and Solemnities of Cycles A, B, and C.*[6] Each intercession consists of an introduction, five biddings, and concluding prayer. Although many authors contributed to the book, all the prayers are similar in form and style.

Like the Canadian book, Roman Catholic sources can form the basis for intercessions in Episcopal liturgies. The lectionaries of the two churches are almost identical, with only minor differences between Roman and Episcopal readings.

Ecumenical Churches

Another ecumenical resource is *Intercession for the Christian People*, edited by Gail Ramshaw.[7] Designed for Roman, Episcopal, and Lutheran lectionaries, the book provides prayers of the people for every Sunday in cycles A, B, and C and for various major holy days. Each intercession includes a brief introduction, several biddings (addressed to the people) or petitions (addressed to God), and a concluding prayer; there is also provision for other biddings or petitions. The various elements carry out the content and meaning of the readings of the day. Since more than fifty authors contributed to the collection, it is not surprising that the many forms differ in style, structure, and tone (unlike the Roman Catholic collection).

The prayers in these and other books may be used as written, perhaps with adaptations, or as models. Those who prefer to write their own prayers for their own time and place may find it useful to look at how others compose intercessions for each Sunday and feast.

---

6   New York: Pueblo Publishing Co., 1977. For other widely used Roman Catholic sources, see the catalog of The Liturgical Press, P.O. Box 7500, Collegeville, MN 56321.

7   New York: Pueblo Publishing Co., 1988.

B. Composing the General Intercessions

Because the intercessions of the eucharist are prayers of the *people*, they belong to the assembly. The assembly hears them, sings them, and offers them to God. They are a community enterprise, a communal discussion with God about problems we want God to solve. This does not mean, however, that many people need to have a hand in composing the prayers. By necessity and good sense, either one person or a committee of modest size usually drafts the intercessions.

If one person writes the prayers, the person should appear to the assembly as an authority in prayer—one who prays daily (and thus can pray on Sunday), and one who is skilled in the structure and content of liturgical composition. The writer of the prayers should be able to articulate for the assembly what it wants to pray week by week, and should know *what* to pray and *how* to pray.

If a committee writes the prayers, the committee also needs the authority of the assembly to compose its intercessions. It should be small and harmonious, able to work as a group, and sensitive to the needs, concerns, and hopes of others. The group may contain those who work with the poor, sick, and other needy persons; its members should at least be aware of those in need in the local community. They should also be aware of concerns about the nation and the world. Week by week, they should listen to the assembly, hearing the voices of the faithful, preparing to pray as the people gather. They should know *what* to pray.

The members of the committee should receive training in prayer. They should experience liturgical and personal prayer. They should be thoroughly familiar with the forms and language they are to use. They should have a clear sense of the role of prayer in their own lives and in the church. If they pray daily, they will have the materials to pray on Sunday. At least one of them should be skilled in writing, to provide the actual drafting of the prayers. They should know *how* to pray.

Many congregations have deacons. As ordained ministers traditionally entrusted with leading intercession, deacons appropriately take part in designing the prayers. A deacon may lead the committee, or one or more of the deacons of the congregation may sit as members of the committee. A committee to write prayers of intercession might operate like this:

> On Sunday morning, an hour before the main service, three parishioners meet to draft the prayers of the people. Having already studied the lectionary readings, they pray for guidance.

For fifteen minutes they discuss the parish family, the community, and the world. Who are the sick, those celebrating birthdays, baptismal days, and wedding anniversaries, those with other needs and concerns? What was in the morning paper, those calamities and major events that will be on everyone's mind?

They share a few ideas about the main thrust of the prayers. They suggest the content and wording of two or three biddings. Then two of them leave the room, and the remaining person writes the intercessions of the day, following one of the forms in the prayer book.

Six Principles of Composition

In composing the general intercessions for a Sunday morning liturgy, the person or committee should consider each of the following six principles.

1. Cover six categories

The general intercessions include six categories of subject matter:
- The church;
- The nation and all in authority (in Canada, the queen);
- The world;
- The local community;
- Those in need;
- The dead.

A congregation should cover these topics in full on Sundays and major feasts, and may condense them on weekdays and other occasions. Even when omitting topics, the assembly is always to pray inclusively for the church and the world.

2. Cover general topics

The prayers of the people are *general* intercessions, extensive in coverage, broad rather than narrow. We ask God's mercy on all those in need in the church and the world. Though we may want to include specific names and local concerns, we do so with restraint. Except on special occasions, such as weddings and funerals, it is better to announce special intentions before the intercessions—and then briefly and selectively.

If we intercede in depth during the week as individuals and as groups, on Sunday morning we do not need to read every name on every prayer list. A period of silence, before or during the prayers, will give all those present the opportunity to offer their own names and concerns, silently or aloud, and even simultaneously.

The general nature of the intercessions makes them unsuitable for advancing social, political, and religious causes. Keep the prayers inclusive. Never use them to preach to the congregation, to correct their thoughts and behavior, or to praise friends and denounce enemies. While cries for mercy imply the need for peace and justice in particular situations, the proper place for a homily is the sermon.

3. Emphasize intercession

The prayers of the people are *intercessions*, entreaties that call on God to help others. Primarily they ask God to relieve needs, remedy concerns, and fulfill hopes. Although several forms (especially II and VI) provide for thanksgiving, the real business of the prayers of the people is intercession. If thanksgiving occurs in another part of the liturgy, or in a separate place, the intercessions will be more clearly intercessory. (There are other logical places for specific thanksgivings, silent or aloud. One is immediately before the Great Thanksgiving; another is at the end of communion.)

4. Let the people pray

The general intercessions are prayers of the *people*, the common supplications of the gathered faithful. It is important that all the people pray earnestly, not merely assent to a leader's extensive prayer. In the early or classic form of intercession, a leader addresses the people, reminding them of topics, and the people respond with a formula, such as "Lord, have mercy," or with a significant period of silent prayer (Forms I and II). In a more recent form, a leader invokes God in terms such as "Father, we pray for...," and the people complete the prayer (Form III).

There is a fundamental difference between the two forms. In the first the leader's ministry is diaconal: a herald or messenger announces topics and encourages the assembly to pray for them. In the second it is priestly: someone offers petitions and simultaneously stands with the assembly in prayer. The first type is especially appropriate when deacons lead the prayers; other baptized persons may use either form.

Forms in which the leader does most of the praying while the people listen, or in which the people's response is a single "Amen," can remove the people from their priestly role as those who offer the petitions. Whatever form of intercession is chosen, the people need to have an active, substantial part.

5. Keep the biddings short and simple

In the classic diaconal litany, the biddings are normally short and simple. Brief biddings are easy to follow and help the people to grasp the topic. It is helpful if all the biddings are of the same liturgical type and follow a common grammatical structure. Brevity applies also to the number of biddings: a sensible number is four or five on weekdays, and six to twelve on Sundays and major feasts.

Petitions addressed by the leader to God should also be short and simple. Modern liturgical speech avoids verbosity and addresses God directly and plainly.

6. Keep the responses short and uniform

If the responses are short and uniform, the people will find them easy to remember and pray. Long or variable responses require people to read from a book or piece of paper. Short, unchanging responses allow them to look up and see the leader and each other, the altar, a cross, an icon, and other aids to prayer. They are free to hold hands, raise them in prayer, and even move about (as in a circle).

Structure of Biddings

A litany is a series of invocations or supplications to which the people respond with a brief entreaty. The statements are usually in the form of
> (1) biddings addressed to the people, or
> (2) petitions or prayers addressed to God.

The classic diaconal litany consists of biddings or topics, which the leader announces to the people.

The biddings normally are constructed in one of three ways:
> • "For [persons or concerns]..."
> *Two or more "for" phrases on similar topics may be strung together in one bidding.*
> • "That [intention]..."
> *Normally there is only one "that" phrase in each bidding.*
> • "For [persons and concerns]..., that [intention]..."
> *Within this complex structure, each bidding should be kept as simple as possible.*

Biddings beginning with "For" may be introduced with a phrase such as "Let us pray for" or "I ask your prayers for." If the leader bids prayer at the beginning, there is no need to end with a "let us pray" formula.

Biddings may end with a phrase such as "let us pray to the Lord," "let us pray," or "we pray." The ending formula alerts the people for their response. In Form V the biddings begin with a message but end with prayer: "we pray to you, O Lord." If the leader sings the biddings, there may be no need for an ending formula. The melodic cadence at the end will let the people know when to respond.

For a brief lesson in composing biddings and responses, see *Supplemental Liturgical Materials*, pages 33-34. Using several examples, the book shows how to construct litanies based on Forms I and V with inclusive language. Thus Form I begins:

> In peace and in faith, let us offer our prayers, saying, "Christ, have mercy."
>
> For peace and tranquillity in the world, and for the salvation of all, let us pray.
>
> For *N.* our Presiding Bishop, for *N.(N.)* our own Bishop(s), and for all the People of God, let us pray.

Form V begins:

> We pray to you, O Christ our God, saying, "Christ, have mercy" (or *"Christe eleison"*).
>
> For the Church of God in every place, that it may persevere in faith and hope, we pray to you.
>
> For all who minister in your Church, (especially _____,) that they may have grace to build up your people in love, we pray to you.[8]

Structure of Petitions

The other main type of litany consists of a series of short prayers. In designing such a litany, the best guide is the collect. In the western church most collects have three parts: an address to God (often including divine attributes), a request that God do such and such, and a statement of the expected result. A well-known example is the collect of the Easter Vigil:

> O God, who made this most holy night to shine with the glory of the Lord's resurrection: Stir up in your Church that Spirit of adoption which is given to us in Baptism, that we, being renewed both in body and mind, may worship you in sincerity and truth; through Jesus Christ our Lord, who lives and

---

8 *Supplemental Liturgical Materials* (New York: The Church Hymnal Corp., 1991), 33-34. Reprinted by permission of the publisher.

reigns with you, in the unity of the Holy Spirit, one God, now and for ever.
(BCP 295; see BAS 329)

In a litany of short prayers each petition uses one or more of the three parts.
The first petition frequently mentions God by name ("Grant, Almighty God,
that"), and subsequent petitions usually ask directly for a favor ("Guide," "Give,"
"Bless"). A petition may ask for both favor and result ("Grant...that"), or a
petition may begin with the result ("That"). The first two petitions of Form IV
illustrate the technique:

> Grant, Almighty God, that all who confess your Name may be united in your
> truth, live together in your love, and reveal your glory in the world.
> Guide the people of this land, and of all the nations, in the ways of justice
> and peace; that we may honor one another and serve the common good.
> (BCP 388)

As in Form VI, a litany may start with an address to God ("we pray to you, Lord
God") and continue with "For" petitions. In all litanies of short prayers, the
people's response may suggest a result ("That") or simply respond to the leader's
call for God's mercy ("Hear our prayer").

Composing the Introduction

> The Celebrant may introduce the Prayers with a sentence of invitation related
> to the occasion, or the season, or the Proper of the Day. (BCP 383)

The invitation is not a miniature homily or prayer but "a sentence" (or no more
than two or three short sentences), brief and addressed to the people. It calls the
people to spiritual arms, inviting them to pray earnestly. It links their intercession
to the readings, season, or occasion, and therefore to the preaching of the gospel.
This is an opportunity for the presider to summarize the sermon and point it
forward into the congregation's life of prayer and action. At the midnight mass
of Christmas, for example, the presider might say:

> At this solemn hour of midnight we join the angels and celebrate with joy
> the birth of Jesus from the womb of Mary. Let us offer prayers to God who
> gives new birth to sons and daughters in every place.

Although the normal inviter is the presider, the prayer book does not prevent
other persons from saying the invitation. It even gives a prominent example in
which others say it. Before the solemn intercessions of Good Friday, "the Deacon,

or other person appointed," calls on the people of God to pray "for people everywhere according to their needs" (BCP 277; see BAS 309). Besides the presider, appropriate persons to offer the invitation are the preacher, deacons, and other leaders of the intercessions.

Except on Good Friday, the Canadian prayer book does not provide for introductions to litanies. It suggests that a cantor begin by singing the response (BAS 110).

Composing the Collect

The prayer book directs the presiding bishop or priest to conclude the general intercessions with a collect. It mentions four types:

(a) a Collect appropriate to the Season or occasion being celebrated;

(b) a Collect expressive of some special need in the life of the local congregation;

(c) a Collect for the mission of the Church;

(d) a general Collect. (BCP 394)

The prayer book then provides eight general collects that, like the six forms of intercession, are examples and models of concluding prayers (BCP 394–395). The first five, in which we ask God to hear our prayers and accept our petitions, are suitable for ordinary use. The last three illustrate other possible purposes. The sixth collect, addressed to Christ and originally a private prayer of the priest in the Sarum rite, points forward to the kiss of peace. The seventh collect illustrates a seasonal theme (Advent), and the eighth links our earthly intercessions with the communion of saints.

The collect serves mainly to *collect* and summarize the people's intentions. Especially during the Season After Pentecost—the ordinary (or green) time of the church year—it refers specifically to the petitions and may repeat an image or theme in the readings. During Advent, Christmas, Epiphany, Lent, and Easter, the collect uses a seasonal motif. On special occasions it usually reflects the event being celebrated.

The collect is clearly presidential, and no other person sings or says this prayer. Thus the bishop or presiding priest may wish to select or compose the prayer, or at least offer advice in its creation.

The collect is a short, formal prayer, which normally follows one of three types, though two or three types may be mixed in one prayer:

(1) the traditional western collect ending with a brief formula, such as "through Jesus Christ our Lord";

(2) Jewish blessings beginning "Blessed are you" and perhaps ending "Glory to you for ever"; and

(3) Eastern Orthodox prayers ending with a Trinitarian doxology (see BCP 391).

The Canadian book does not require a collect after each litany. It provides a collect for Litany 1, collects within Litany 17, and a collect for Litany 18. After the litanies it prints thirteen collects (BAS 111, 124-127, 130-132).

C. Praying the General Intercessions

Ministers of the Intercessions

The bishop or presbyter who presides at the liturgy normally gives the invitation; a deacon or other leader of the intercessions may also fill this function.

When the intercessions are a diaconal litany, normally a deacon announces the biddings; other designated persons (but not a bishop or priest) may also function as leader. This is not a function to win or lose in a parish battle. Deacons lead intercession because they are ordained as the messengers and heralds of the church. The congregation may also have a strong commitment to the leadership of other baptized persons in liturgy. Deacons and other leaders should find ways to cooperate in the intercessions, alternating biddings and otherwise sharing. Preferably the leaders of intercession are those who lead, encourage, and prompt the people in service to those in need.

When the intercessions take the form of petitions addressed to God, the appropriate leader is a baptized member of the assembly, not ordained but functioning in a priestly role. The congregation should recognize and endorse the leadership of this person.

As their rightful act of intercession, the people make the responses. The presider sums up with a collect, to which the people respond, "Amen."

Performance

After the invitation the leader may read, or invite others to read, a few special intentions. (They may also read special intentions at the end of the prayers, or within them.) Special topics may include the universal church, the diocese, the parish, the world, and the local community. Many congregations read lists of members celebrating baptismal days and wedding anniversaries during the coming week, the seriously ill, and the dead. For this purpose there may be a large book of remembrances, with blank pages for names and concerns. Worshipers may tell the leader beforehand about specific names or write them down. It is not necessary to read every name and concern suggested. Those read should be moderate in number, concentrating on critical needs.

After the special intentions, or elsewhere, the leader may invite the people to recall their daily prayers and offer their own names silently or aloud. In some places the leader may need to urge the people to participate, while in other places the leader may need to restrain them. After giving them a little time (but not too long) the leader begins the formal biddings.

The leader may use one of two gestures during the prayers: hands folded or raised in prayer. To emphasize the public nature of intercessory prayer, the leader may extend hands, palms turned forward and upward, in the ancient *orans* or prayer gesture. (According to scripture and ancient custom, the people also may lift their hands in prayer.) To hold the gesture, the leader may need to memorize the biddings, or someone else may hold the book. In another gesture, this one from eastern liturgies, a deacon may hold the diaconal stole about a foot from the end, using three fingers of the right hand.

During the prayers the leader or a server may gently swing a censer, with "a great quantity of incense to offer with the prayers of all the saints" (Revelation 8:3), or someone may put grains of incense on charcoal burning in a brazier.

When the intercessions take the form of a litany, it is often desirable to sing them. The use of music helps to form the community and calls it to discipleship and communion. Simple melodies appear in the Hymnal at S106 (Form I), S107 (Form III), S108 (Form IV), and S109 (Form V), and in the Service Music Appendix at S362 (Form II) and S363 (Form VI). For the responses, congregations may try other melodies from traditional plainchant or modern sources, such as Taizé. In the Canadian book, music for responses to the litanies is provided in an appendix (BAS 915-917).[9]

During the litany the leader sings each bidding or at least the ending formula. Different persons may sing biddings and endings in rotation. Typically each bidding is sung on one note, with an inflection at the end. In another method, the leader reads the biddings (or several leaders read them), and a song leader chants an ending formula, such as "let us pray to the Lord." If the congregation is unfamiliar with the chanted response, the leader (or someone else) may sing it before the litany. The people repeat it before the first bidding.

---

9 For examples of music in litanies, see chapter 11, pages 126-131.

Harmony helps to improve the quality of the singing and the sense of unity in the assembly. At the end of each bidding the people may sing "Lord, have mercy" (or other response) in four parts (as in Hymnal S106, BAS 915). They may hum in parts during the next bidding, helping to keep the leader on pitch, and they may overlap the word "Lord" with the "Lord" that ends each bidding.

Another way to overlap the leader's chant is to sing "Lord, have mercy" after the first bidding (in unison or in parts), slowly and repeatedly, while the leader sings all the biddings. The leader may slow or pause, change pace, and let the people catch up. To accomplish this, the congregation may chant a simple *Kyrie eleison* or a Slavonic chant, such as the *Gospodi pomiluj* (Lord, have mercy) sung at *Taizé*.[10]

The leader may need copies of the text, but the congregation that has rehearsed the music or sung it week after week is free to look, listen, pray, and sing.

The choice of the place from which the prayers are led should suit the worship space and the needs of the congregation. A formal setting usually contains two main places to lead the prayers:

> • *The lectern (ambo) or pulpit.* The deacon or other leader faces the people. This is the place common in the western church.
> • *The midst, or the head, of the congregation.* The deacon or other leader may begin by facing the people (or by facing away from the altar). After the special intentions the leader turns to face the altar. This is the place common in the eastern church.

In an informal setting the people may face the place of the word or form a circle around the altar. They may focus on an icon or another point of prayer. They may stand where they are. The presider may stand on one side of the assembly (the *east* side) or at the chair. The leader may stand on the opposite side, or among the people, or beside the presider, or at an ambo. The assembly may even be in movement, perhaps from the word place to the table place.

---

10 *Songs & Prayers from Taizé* (Chicago: GIA Publications, 1991), no. 7.

5

Day by Day

<hr>

Although our life in Christ becomes most vital and focused when we gather on Sunday and major feasts, we also celebrate Christ every day of the week, through acts of prayer at many times and in many places. Day by day we adore and praise God, give thanks, confess our sins, ask for mercy, and intercede for others. We do these things because we are a baptized people. At our baptism we enter a life of habitual, continual prayer, which takes place both in private and in community.

Intercession in daily prayer trains us for intercession in the Sunday eucharist. It gives us the materials, the skills, the habit of prayer, as through intimate talk we rehearse our community conversation with God. This daily prayer stands on its own and has its own value. Morning and evening we make our sacrifice of praise and intercession to the living God through Jesus Christ.

Prayer in Private

Throughout the centuries, the prime hours of prayer have been sunrise and sunset. We rise and bless God, lift our voices in praise with all the works of creation, and pray "that our lives may proclaim your goodness, our works give you honor, and our voices praise you for ever" (BAS 784). As the day ends, we light the lamps of evening, praise God for the light of Christ, and give thanks for all the blessings we have received during the day. Other hours of prayer are also common—especially noon and bedtime—but morning and evening are the main ones, hallowed by ancient tradition and the rhythm of daily life in sleeping and waking, eating, working, and resting.

When daily prayer takes place regularly, normally it includes intercession. Since the early centuries, Christian prayer at sunrise and sunset has embraced two principal motifs: praise and intercession. Having approached God with praise, we dare to ask for God's mercy.

It is always desirable for Christians to gather for prayer. Often, however, in the clutter of our lives or in circumstances of isolation we find neither the time nor the means to assemble. Then we pray alone. Those who have much time at their disposal can give prayer the time it deserves, and prayer plays a large part in their lives. Those who have less time need to see the importance of prayer, to find moments for prayer, and to guard their prayer from interruption.

Many Episcopalians who pray alone use the daily office in the *Book of Common Prayer*, which contains psalms, canticles, readings, intercessions, and other prayers. Others use a section called "Daily Devotions for Individuals and Families" (BCP 136-140), which follow the structure of the daily office. These devotions are especially suitable for individuals. After a psalm or canticle of praise and a brief reading, they allow prayers "for ourselves and others." They also allow alterations and substitutions, including devotional materials from other sources. Thus they provide the basic forms for all daily prayer.

Similarly, many Canadian Anglicans use the divine office in the *Book of Alternative Services*, which has liturgies for morning, midday, evening (with a service of light), and Saturday evening. A separate section of "Home Prayers" for groups or families (BAS 685-697) contains a litany of intercession. The home prayers are designed for use at the evening meal but can be adapted for other times.

Times of Prayer

At different hours of the day intercessory prayer deals with different topics. Morning prayer looks forward to the new day. It greets the rising sun, symbol of the risen Christ, and gathers into its scope all those who have risen to work, study, and play during the coming day. Intercessions in the morning may be as inclusive as those in the eucharist, recalling all those in need in the church and the world. Those praying alone may anticipate those whom they will meet or talk with during the next twenty-four hours, mention their names, and ask God to have mercy on them. Other topics at this hour are God's works of creation and issues of the environment.

If a person also prays at noon, or at other times during the daylight hours, intercessions may develop the topics of morning prayer. They may reflect the time of day, especially the hours of Christ's passion and death on the cross. They may concentrate on those who are working or traveling, on the nations of the world, and on issues of justice and peace. Reflecting the busy-ness of the world, the intercessions may deal with commerce, agriculture, government, and the like. (If there is no prayer at noon, these topics may be dealt with at morning prayer.)

Evening prayer looks backward to the day that is past, giving thanks and remembering. This is the hour when families and friends gather, eat, and socialize, when workers return home and students come back from school. Even when one prays alone, it is the hour of family prayer. The main topic of intercessory prayer may be the family—a circle around oneself that is both vertical and horizontal, including parents and grandparents, husbands and wives, children, grandchildren and great-grandchildren, aunts, uncles, cousins, nieces and nephews, friends, the living and the dead—the whole panorama of relationships summed up by the term *extended family*.

In the evening those praying alone may recall persons they have encountered or talked with during the day. Our commerce and exchanges during the day have given us a satchel of names and concerns, which we bring home with us. In our evening intercessions we empty our pockets, gather our affairs into the circle of our family life, and offer them to God.

If a person prays at bedtime, especially using the liturgy known as compline (from the Latin *completa* or "complete"), intercessions may concentrate on those who are in peril or danger during the night, who work while others sleep, who must remain awake. It is an appropriate time to pray for the dying and the dead, and for the salvation of oneself. (If there is no prayer at bedtime, we may deal with these topics at evening prayer.)

Places of Prayer

When we pray alone, it helps to find a suitable setting, a quiet place that welcomes us and puts us at ease. We stand or sit, walk or ride, kneel or lie down, perhaps on a rug (lying face down is an ancient posture for private prayer). We breathe in a regular pattern and use the same words repeatedly ("Lord, have mercy"). Making sure the lighting is subdued and indirect, we may use an icon, statue, or candle to help us focus our prayer. We imagine scenes in scripture, and we open our hearts to the breath of God. In our relaxation we can concentrate on prayer.

Sometimes, however, we have little opportunity to withdraw into a place of private prayer. We must make our intercessions and other prayers while getting dressed, brushing our teeth, traveling to and from work, doing chores, or preparing supper. We may be in the midst of work, in an office or on a job site, able to find only a minute or two to gather our thoughts and offer names to God.

In these instances, we keep the intercessions simple, recall as many names and concerns as we can, and do not worry about omissions. "Lord, have mercy on..." (and we name them). In private prayer it is appropriate to address God directly, especially Jesus. "Lord Jesus Christ, Son of God, have mercy on me a sinner, and also have mercy on..." (adding names). If we feel like singing our prayers, our song expresses the offering of ourselves to God.

Prayer in Community

Though intercession alone is desirable, intercession in community is preferable. A text in the fourth century instructs the people:

> Since you are members of Christ...assemble every day, morning and evening, singing and praying in the house of the Lord.[1]

Because Christians are members of the body of Christ even when they pray alone, the topics used by individuals at morning and evening, and other hours, are the same topics that are used by groups within the Christian community. Their prayer for the church and the world each day should include a broad range of subject matter appropriate to sunrise, sunset, or any other hour of prayer.

Daily prayer in families and other close groups lies at the heart of Christian life. They may use the daily office, the Episcopal Daily Devotions, the Canadian Home Prayers, or other forms of daily prayer designed for morning and evening. They may shorten or alter the office, if it provides for both praise and intercession.

The Daily Office
The normal daily prayer for the gathered Christian community in the Episcopal Church is the daily office in the *Book of Common Prayer* (BCP 35-135; see BAS 47-71). The daily office includes morning prayer and evening prayer, perhaps supplemented by noonday prayer and compline. These are monastic offices,

---

1 W. Jardine Grisbrooke, ed., *The Liturgical Portions of the Apostolic Constitutions: A Text for Students*, Alcuin/GROW Liturgical Study 13-14 (Bramcote, Notts.: Grove Books Ltd., 1990), 54.

descended from liturgies that were developed in the fourth century and brought to England by Benedictine monks. Archbishop Thomas Cranmer revised these offices as matins and evensong. The 1979 prayer book also contains a version of the ancient cathedral (or popular) office called An Order of Worship for the Evening.

Morning Prayer and Evening Prayer

Intercession in the Episcopal daily offices of morning prayer and evening prayer occurs in the closing section called "The Prayers" and consists of three parts: a choice of two suffrages, a choice of collects, and other intercessions. In morning prayer there are two suffrages, both consisting of versicles and responses taken from the psalms. In the first the petitions cover clergy and people, world and nation, poor and needy, and ourselves. In the second they call for love and mercy on the people of God. *Supplemental Liturgical Materials* includes another set of suffrages for morning prayer, drawn from the psalms (SLM 29).

In evening prayer the first set of suffrages is the same as the first set in morning prayer. The second set is a version of the ancient litany still used in Eastern Orthodox vespers. It asks for a peaceful evening, the guidance of angels, pardon of sins, peace in the church and the world, and a Christian death.

The collects include prayers for the mission of the church. In the morning these cover the faithful and all the peoples of the earth; in the evening they also include "those who work, or watch, or weep this night," and those who sleep.

Following the collects, both offices provide for "authorized intercessions and thanksgivings." What makes an intercession authorized is probably its use by an authorized leader of the assembly. The additional directions note, however, that "opportunity may be given for the members of the congregation to express intentions or objects of prayer and thanksgiving, either at the bidding, or in the course of the prayer; and opportunity may be given for silent prayer" (BCP 142).

Morning prayer and evening prayer in the Canadian office contain a section called "Intercessions and Thanksgivings," followed by the collect, Lord's Prayer, and dismissal. The directions for intercession are similar to those in the eucharist. They call for prayer on six topics, suggest a brief litany from a collection elsewhere in the book, and allow the litanies to be modified "in accordance with local need, or extempore forms of prayer may be used" (BAS 53, 70).

The Order of Worship for the Evening (BCP 109-114) may be used as the normal evening prayer, including intercessions, or it may be used as a complete evening office with a "litany, or other suitable devotions" (BCP 113). A simple litany, such as the second suffrages in evening prayer, allows the worshipers to sing biddings and responses.

The Canadian Service of Light, which also may serve as the opening of evening prayer, contains no intercessions.

Noonday Prayer

The noonday office (BCP 103-107) has no formal intercessions. Among its choice of collects are those for ourselves, all peoples, all nations, and the church. Just before the dismissal the office suggests that "free intercessions may be offered" (BCP 107).

Similarly, the Canadian midday liturgy provides for "intercessions and thanksgivings" (BAS 58).

Compline

Compline (BCP 127-135) includes collects for the sick and dying, those who sleep, and those who work during the night. The office adds: "Silence may be kept, and free intercessions and thanksgivings may be offered" (BCP 134).

Other Forms for Daily Prayer

The official liturgical books do not exhaust the possibilities for forms of daily prayer used by Episcopalians, Canadian Anglicans, and others. One prayer book widely in use is *Celebrating Common Prayer*, a version of the daily office published by Anglican Franciscans in England.[2] The two main offices of morning prayer and evening prayer include a flexible *Kyrie eleison*, which "may be used as responses to intercession." As a further aid, the book contains twenty-three litanies of many types, some seasonal, some topical, and some occasional, and suggests the use of other sources.

Another source available to Episcopalians and Canadian Anglicans is the daily office book of Taizé, *Praise in All Our Days*.[3] Each office is fully printed out, containing its own litany of intercession (often based on scriptural and traditional sources) and a place for free prayer. The value of the Taizé liturgy lies in its ecumenical spirit; the monks suggest it as the contribution of a Christian community for research and use in worship.

---

2 Mowbray, 1992.

3 Mowbray, 1981.

These and other sources provide a variety of materials for intercessory prayer. One does not have to use their offices in their entirety; the intercessions may be borrowed and modified for local needs.

In many places research and experimentation in liturgy are focusing on a revival of the "cathedral" offices which flourished in the early church as Christians in cities gathered in the bishop's church at sunrise and sunset and also celebrated a vigil of the resurrection on Saturday night. These popular services were more lively and dramatic than the more contemplative monastic liturgies, and involved a rich use of symbols—candlelight, incense, chanting, processions, and various ministries. They also provided for extensive intercessions, usually in the form of litanies.[4]

---

4 For sample litanies for morning and evening, especially for "cathedral" liturgies, see pages 109-111.

6

Season by Season

J ust as sunrise and sunset and the other hours of the day call for different emphases, styles, and topics of intercessory prayer, the seasons of the church year require distinct and particular expressions of prayer. Like all other types of prayer, intercession bears the marks of each season. Our conversation with God dances to the rhythm of God's world, morning and evening, hot and cold, planting and harvesting, birth and death, remorse and forgiveness, expectancy and completion, sadness and joy. So we make our way through the spiral of God's creation toward ultimate union with Christ.

Advent

For a guide to intercession in Advent, there is no better source than the collect of the first Sunday of Advent, a prayer infused with the imagery and spirit of scripture (see Romans 13:12):

> Almighty God, give us grace to cast away the works of darkness, and put on the armor of light, now in the time of this mortal life in which your Son Jesus Christ came to visit us in great humility; that in the last day, when he shall come again in his glorious majesty to judge both the living and the dead, we may rise to the life immortal; through him who lives and reigns with you and the Holy Spirit, one God, now and for ever.

The main themes of Advent are the first coming and the second coming. Thus the primary word of the season is *come*, and we cry with urgency: "Come, O Lord, and save us." Intercessions might call for the coming of Jesus Christ, Wisdom, Emmanuel, peace in the world, the kingdom of God, and the unity of all peoples.

In the northern hemisphere Advent is a time of short days, when the darkness of night threatens to overcome the brightness of day. Just before Christmas the shortening of day stops and the process begins slowly to reverse itself. Darkness threatens prison and death, but the expectation of light promises freedom and life. Intercessions may incorporate the imagery of darkness and light as they call for deliverance.

One way to use this imagery is to pray the traditional O Antiphons as concluding collects. The O Antiphons are familiar to Episcopalians and other Anglicans as the verses in the hymn "O come, O come, Emmanuel" (Hymn 56). All of these antiphons deal with themes of coming and saving. One in particular develops the imagery of light:

O Rising Sun,
> brightness of light eternal,
>> sun of justice,
> come and shine on those who sit in darkness
>> and the shadow of death.

The Canadian book prints the O Antiphons as petitions in an Advent litany (BAS 119-120).[1]

Advent is the season of messages and warnings, of preparation and pregnancy, of stirring up and purifying, of Isaiah, John the Baptist, and Mary the God-bearer. These themes and persons are expressed in the collects and readings of the Sundays of Advent. It is a season of great hymns reflecting the mystery of Christ, from the darkness of creation to the dawn of the next age: "Creator of the stars of night" (Hymn 60) and "The King shall come when morning dawns" (Hymn 73). All these themes and images provide rich materials for the writers and leaders of intercession.[2]

Many places celebrate an Advent Festival of Lessons and Carols, usually in the evening. The *Book of Occasional Services* contains traditional and contemporary versions of the monologue bidding prayer that opens this service from the Church of England (BOS 29-31). These intercessions include petitions for the needs of the world, peace and goodwill, the mission and unity of the church, the poor, and

---

1   For another translation, with a doxology at the end of each antiphon, see pages 115-116.

2   For a sample Advent litany, see pages 114-116.

other persons in need. They conclude with a remembrance of the "pure and lowly Mother" of God and of all who have died. The people respond with the Lord's Prayer.[3]

Christmas and Epiphany

The seasons of the incarnation of Christ are a series of festivals and observances. They begin with the eve of Christmas Day and last until the Epiphany and the Baptism of Christ and even, in year C, until the Second Sunday after the Epiphany, when the Johannine gospel is about the wedding in Cana. (Some will argue that Candlemas and even the entire post-Epiphany time until Ash Wednesday belong to the incarnational cycle.)

Intercessions during this season may reflect the gradually unfolding themes of the incarnation emphasized by the collects and readings. For example, we may begin the intercessory biddings with an appropriate "by" phrase. At midnight mass: "By the birth of the timeless Son of God in the womb of the Virgin Mary...." On the first Sunday of Christmas: "By the wedding of the human and divine natures in Christ Jesus...."

The midnight eucharist holds a special place in the Christmas season. Reflecting the gospel, the intercessions may mention that we are joining our voices with the angels. If there are celebrations on Christmas Day, the early or dawn eucharist may mention the shepherds, and the late or day service the Word made flesh.

On every feast of these seasons, each intercession draws its inspiration from a different aspect of the incarnation. The Epiphany calls for a reference to "the manifestation of the King of the Jews to the shepherds and the magi." On the Sunday after, we may refer to "the baptism of the Son of God in the river Jordan." Since the Epiphany is a triple mystery, with a threefold manifestation combining the visit of the magi, the baptism in the Jordan, and the miracle at Cana, we may also mention in our prayers "the water made wine at Cana of Galilee."

Because the mystery of the incarnation calls for us to raise our voices in high praise with the angels, the people may respond to petitions, "Hear us, Lord of glory." In a season marked by the coming of the Prince of peace, we may pray, "Lord, grant us peace."[4]

---

3 For the Canadian treatment, see *Occasional Celebrations*, pages 11-12.

4 For a sample litany at Christmas, Epiphany, and Baptism, see pages 116-117. The Canadian litany for the incarnation consists of a series of invocations, BAS 120-121.

The Christmas Festival of Lessons and Carols in the *Book of Occasional Services* is similar to the one for Advent. For the intercessions, see pages 36–38, and *Occasional Celebrations*, pages 22–23.

Some congregations sanctify the night of December 31 with a Service for New Year's Eve (BOS 40–44). This may conclude with the Great Litany or another form of intercession. January 1 is an occasion to pray for newborn children and their naming. In places where the parish priest blesses the homes of parishioners on the Feast of the Epiphany or during the week following, the intercessions may include their names.

The Weeks After the Epiphany

The weeks after the Epiphany and the Baptism of Christ have an ambiguous personality, both ordinary and epiphanal. Some Sundays continue the theme of the manifestation of Jesus; on the last Sunday the gospel tells the story of Christ's transfiguration. Other Sundays emphasize calling and sending. This is a good time to pray for the mission of the church—its sending forth—and for the ministry of those whom God and the church send.

Candlemas (February 2) falls within this time. This is an occasion to pray for children, to ask that their parents or others bring them into the Christian assembly.

Lent

Ash Wednesday

Among all the holy days, Ash Wednesday is the most peculiar from the perspective of intercessory prayer. The church asks us to turn our thoughts to our own sinful nature and to "the sins of all who are penitent." There is no provision for the people to pray for the needs of others. Instead, the presider leads the people in a Litany of Penitence, which is different from intercession.

The Sundays in Lent

During Lent the intercessions take their material from the themes of the season and the readings of each day. Lent has two purposes: preparation for the celebration of the paschal feast by penitence and fasting, and restoration of notorious sinners to the communion of the church by penitence and forgiveness. Thus Lent looks both forward to resurrection and new life, and backward to sin, destruction, and death.

Woven into this thematic design is an increasingly important source of Lenten intercessions, the catechumenate. In this ancient process adult candidates underwent their final preparation for baptism at the Easter Vigil. Places that have restored the catechumenate pray for their candidates by name throughout Lent. In the early church catechumens were dismissed just before the general intercessions: without baptism they could not share in the royal priesthood of offering petitions to God. Many places today have restored this ancient custom.

In a parallel process to the catechumenate, during Lent some mature adults prepare to reaffirm their baptismal vows at the Easter Vigil. Where this preparation takes place, the assembly also prays for these candidates by name in the intercessions each Sunday.

On the first Sunday in Lent there are two main possibilities for intercession:

(1) When there are candidates for baptism or renewal of baptismal vows, a deacon or another person leads a special litany (in the style of a classic litany), which includes biddings for the candidates and their teachers, sponsors, families, and friends (BOS 122-123).

(2) When there are no candidates for baptism, it is appropriate to sing or say the Great Litany just before the eucharist, perhaps during a procession (BCP 148-153). Alternatively, the congregation may use a litany of intercession as on any other Sunday.

If the Great Litany is not used on the first Sunday in Lent, it may take place on the second Sunday or on any other Sunday. On all the Sundays in Lent the candidates and their sponsors are named in the intercessions (BOS 124).

As in all other seasons, the collects and readings in Lent guide us with themes and images for intercession. It is important that our prayers reflect the spirit of the holy fast of Lent. Carrying out the message of Ash Wednesday, we may ask for the grace "to pray, fast, and give alms." We may pray for those who fast involuntarily and for those who receive alms, the hungry and poor of the world and our community.

On the first Sunday in Lent, having heard of the temptation of Christ, we may pray for "the destruction of demonic powers." In the middle of Lent the mood changes. As we approach Easter, the readings shift from penitence and fasting to images of baptism and eucharist, and we adjust our prayers to reflect the approaching paschal feast. We may pray for those who hunger and thirst for righteousness, those who, like the Samaritan woman at the well, seek the living water of Spirit and truth.

There are other ways to use scripture in the intercessions during Lent. The Ten Commandments, if read as part of the penitential order (BCP 317-318, 350), offer an opportunity to pray for faith in God, for parents, and for the victims of murder, adultery, theft, false witness, and covetousness (and for those who commit such crimes).

Although Matthew 25:31-46 (the Judgment of Christ) does not appear in the Sunday lectionary in Lent, its recurring list of six categories of need provides material for Lenten prayer. Each Sunday our intercessions may focus on one category: the hungry, the thirsty, strangers, the naked, the sick, or those in prison—not necessarily in that order.[5]

Holy Week

Palm Sunday
On the Sunday of the Passion, and throughout Holy Week, it is appropriate to pray for those accused of crimes, those in the court system, prisoners, those condemned to death, and those who have died by execution. We also may pray for accusers, witnesses, judges, guards, and executors, and for victims of crime. In our prayers there is no preference for the innocent over the guilty, for Christ hangs on the cross with two criminals, all three dying as equals.

Maundy Thursday
The sacred triduum (three days) of the paschal feast begins with this evening liturgy. This eucharist incorporates several themes that provide materials for the intercessions. Because the liturgy recalls the Last Supper, we may pray for the hungry, for families and friends who gather for meals, and for all who would like to gather. Because we wash feet in imitation of Christ, we may pray for strangers, travelers, and aliens. Christ gives his disciples a gift of peace, and so we pray for peace in the world and for "peace which the world cannot give." He gives them a new commandment, and we pray for love, for the grace and strength to love one another.

At this liturgy let us not forget to pray urgently for the candidates for baptism as they enter the final days of spiritual and physical cleansing. In places where fasting is practiced, from now until their baptism at the Easter Vigil they will go

---

5 For two examples of Lenten litanies, one for the first three weeks and the other for the last three, see pages 118-120.

with little or no food. The intercessions may also include those preparing for reaffirmation.

Good Friday

The liturgy of Good Friday includes a special form of intercession, the Solemn Collects, a modern version of the prayers of the faithful used in ancient Rome. A deacon "or other person appointed" invites the people to prayer and then sings or says five long biddings; several deacons and others may share in this leadership. A period of silence follows each bidding; the people may be directed to kneel and then to stand. After each bidding the presider sings or says a collect.

Each bidding has a three-part structure: "Let us pray for" introduces a general topic, several "for" phrases elaborate the details, and a "that" clause gives the hoped-for result. The second part—the elaboration of the details—"may be adapted by addition or omission, as appropriate, at the discretion of the Celebrant" (BCP 277). Normally, however, someone else is in charge of the biddings and should not hesitate to make desirable changes. Those preparing for baptism should be named. (The Canadian book does not mention adaptations, BAS 309-313.)

The general topics of the five biddings cover the holy catholic church, all nations and peoples and those in authority, all who suffer and are afflicted, and all who have not received the gospel. The prayers end with a commitment to God in the communion of saints.

These intercessions are especially effective when chanted to the simple preface tone given in the Episcopal altar book. The text includes the traditional chant for the diaconal directions at the silence, in Latin *Flectamus genua* and *Levate*. At the end of each bidding a deacon or someone else directs: "Let us kneel in silent prayer." After a period of silence (perhaps a minute) the same or another person commands: "Arise."

Holy Saturday

The liturgy of this day, a special form of the pro-anaphora, or liturgy of the word, does not include the prayers of the people. Christ among the dead is our only intercessor this day. We keep a holy silence.

Easter

The Great Vigil of Easter

In the early church the first Christian activity of the newly baptized was to join the assembly for the prayers of the people. The *Book of Common Prayer* requires the prayers of the people at the Easter Vigil (BCP 295), following the baptism of the catechumens and the reaffirmation of baptismal vows; the Canadian *Book of Alternative Services* does not say what happens at that point in the Vigil, but the normal baptismal liturgy omits the general intercessions (BAS 162).

The presider or the person who is leading the prayers may begin, "Joined by those who are newly baptized in Christ...." The community should then mention the newly baptized by name and may also include their teachers and sponsors, families, and friends. The prayers will be especially joyful if the newly baptized, their hair still damp and their foreheads glistening with chrism, remain in the full sight of the congregation.

As the most opulent and sensual of all liturgies, the Easter Vigil offers multiple themes and images for intercession. It is queen of feasts, the feast of feasts, a night holier than all other nights. It is the victory of our king, the light of Christ who triumphs over the forces of darkness. We remember God's creation and pray for its salvation. We remember the people of the covenant. We remember Abraham and Moses and all our ancient ancestors of Israel.

Reminded of the escape of the Jewish people from Egypt, we pray for slaves and all in bondage, for their descendants, and for all prisoners, captives, and their families. Reminded of the women who brought myrrh to the empty tomb, we pray for all who approach the risen Christ with faith, reverence, and the fear of God, and for all who witness his resurrection in their lives and ministries.

The Easter Vigil is the marriage supper of the Lamb, a banquet and dance with rich food and pulsating music. In our prayers we may ask to enter the chambers of the wedding feast in heaven.

In their responses, the people may pray not only to the God who has mercy on sinners but also to the "Lord of glory."[6]

The Fifty Days of Easter

The main themes of the Easter Vigil continue during the great fifty days: triumph over sin and death, resurrection of the dead, initiation into the Christian

---

6 For a sample Easter Vigil litany, see pages 120-121.

community. On the seven Sundays of Easter these themes are elaborated with other passages from scripture.

The Sunday of Thomas, for example, presents a vivid image of one who must see the evidence of resurrection before he believes. We may pray for "those who have not seen and yet have come to believe" (John 20:29). Similarly, the story of the road to Emmaus and the statement that "I am the good shepherd" offer opportunities for intercession about the Christian assembly, the eucharist, hunger, helplessness, and ministry.[7]

Rogation Days

A seasonal event that calls for intercession is the Rogation Days on the Monday, Tuesday, and Wednesday before Ascension Day. These are the traditional times to pray for crops, cattle, fisheries, and other sources of food, and even (in some congregations) for all places of work.

Since the word *rogation* comes from a Latin word meaning "ask," this is a suitable time to use the church's most extensive form of intercession, the Great Litany (BCP 148-155, BAS 138-143). It may be sung or said before the eucharist, after the collects of morning prayer and evening prayer, or as a separate liturgy. Following a procession, perhaps around the boundaries of fields and other locations of work, the litany begins as the group enters the church building.

The *Book of Occasional Services* provides three petitions to be inserted in the Great Litany concerning weather, lands, and waters, and all who care for earth, water, and air. If the Great Litany is not used, the *Book of Occasional Services* suggests Form V for the prayers of the people and gives three petitions to insert (BOS 102-103).

Ascension Day

The feast of the Ascension, with the nine days following, has a distinct character, which the prayers may reflect. Although we are still in the Easter season, the themes remind us of Advent, concentrating on the kingship of Christ and on his coming again in power and glory. We may pray especially for the coming of Christ, for all rulers and others in authority, and for the kingdom of God.

On the next Sunday, the seventh in Easter, the intercessions may draw on themes in the high priestly prayer of Jesus in John 17, which supplies the gospel

---

7   For a sample Easter litany, see pages 121-122.

on all three years. One important theme is "that we all may be one, even as the Son and the Father are one."

The Day of Pentecost

On the feast of the Holy Spirit we may pray "for the coming of the Spirit," "for the fire of love," and "for the dove of peace." On the last day the paschal candle burns we may pray again "for the light of Christ" and use other themes and images from the Easter Vigil.

If there are baptisms on this day, the intercessions should mention by name the newly baptized and refer to their teachers, sponsors, families, and friends.

The Season After Pentecost

The "green" Sundays and weeks after Pentecost are commonly known as ordinary time, from the Latin *tempus ordinarii*, numbered days. These weeks after Pentecost are a countdown until Christ returns to stop the clock and start eternal day. Although these numbered days follow no special sequence, there are several clusters of topics and images in the Sunday readings.

In midsummer, when many farmers in the northern hemisphere are harvesting crops, the lectionary in all three years contains gospel readings about sowing and harvesting, boats and fish, bread and wine, food and drink. The sacramental content suggests that we pray for those who hunger and thirst, both physically and spiritually.

In the fall, toward the end of the church year, the readings turn toward the end of time, the kingdom of God, and the judgment of Christ. Especially in November, the month of All Saints and All Souls, we should pray for all who have gone before us.

There are also themes suggested by cultural and seasonal events. May and June contain Sundays devoted to mothers and fathers. In June we may pray for those being married that month and for those celebrating wedding anniversaries. Early July calls for prayers for the United States on its birthday, and if the congregation contains those of foreign heritage, we may also pray for other nations, such as Mexico on Cinco de Mayo (5 May) and France on Bastille Day (14 July). Because all summer is a time of vacations, we pray for those traveling and for those who must stay at home. At the end of summer, at least on the Sunday before Labor Day, we pray for those who work.

Every Sunday in ordinary time celebrates the mystery of Christ, and our prayers of intercession thus draw a connection between the innumerable deaths and births of this world and Christ's death and resurrection. We focus especially on the ministry and teaching of Christ in Galilee, which appears in most of the gospel readings.

Finally, in this season as in every season, to know what to pray we must know not only the readings but the lives of those around us. On every Sunday and weekday, the readings, the preaching, and the needs, concerns, and hopes of the church, the nation, the world, the local community, and all those in need guide our intercessions.

7

Occasion by Occasion

Our lives are marked by the beat of occasional events as well as the rhythm of the weekly and seasonal calendar. We pause to celebrate a marriage, to welcome a newborn child, to baptize a new Christian, to reaffirm baptismal promises, to care for the sick, to bury the dead. As members of the Christian assembly, we order the body of Christ by consecrating bishops, presbyters, and deacons, and we celebrate ministries of many and diverse kinds. Just as the seasons of the church year require their own intercessions, the significant occasions of life in family and church call for prayers that address each event in a distinct and particular way.

Feasts of Saints

Often a saint's day is important in the life of a congregation named after the saint. Other congregations may have a special devotion for a saint because of an icon or statue or another devotional reason. Because those who intercede include the dead and the living, we may ask that our prayers for mercy join with those of the blessed Virgin Mary and all the holy dead in Christ.[1]

---

1   For a sample litany for All Saints' Day or any saint's day, see pages 122–123.

All Souls' Day (November 2) is the traditional occasion for remembering all the dead. In many places it is the custom to read aloud lists of those who have died in the parish or in parishioners' families. This may be done before or during the prayers of the people or during Eucharistic Prayer D. If prayer D is used, at the place for intercessions the presider starts by saying, for example, "Remember the dead of our congregation and families," and then one or more persons (not necessarily priests) read the names. The list, however, should not stretch the liturgy to unreasonable length.

Catechumenate
BOS 112-126 and 132-141

Directions and liturgies for the catechumenate (catechumens are adults preparing for baptism) and the catechumenal process (including reaffirmands, who are mature, baptized persons preparing for reaffirmation of their baptismal vows) are set forth in the *Book of Occasional Services*. As a rule, the intercessions each Sunday should include the names of persons in these two categories, especially those preparing for baptism. Names of catechumens and reaffirmands should appear as separate lists.

Occasional Celebrations does not yet contain the catechumenate, but other sources in the Anglican Church of Canada provide liturgies similar to those in the Episcopal Church.

Baptism
BCP 297-314, BAS 150-165

The rite of baptism in the *Book of Common Prayer* contains two provisions for intercession. One is the special Prayers for the Candidates; the other is the normal (but optional) general intercessions. Unlike the *Book of Common Prayer*, the *Book of Alternative Services* does not allow prayers of the people after a baptism.

In many places the intercessions for the candidates take place while they are moving to the font or just after they have moved there. Thus the intercessions can be a processional chant; the altar book provides music for the petitions and responses. The presider says an introduction to prayer and sings or says a concluding collect. The leader (who may be anyone "appointed," especially a sponsor) sings or says six petitions addressed to God, to which the people respond,

"Lord, hear our prayer." Unlike many other litanies of intercession, this one does not lend itself to adaptation.

At the end of the baptisms and chrismations, the people exchange a sign of peace, and then the prayer book directs that the service continue "with the Prayers of the People or the Offertory of the Eucharist" (BCP 310, but see BAS 162). This rubric has confused many Episcopalians. Should there be intercessions or not? If there are no intercessions, the people may have no chance to pray for those in danger and need. If there are intercessions, should another kiss of peace follow them, as in the normal structure of the eucharist?

One solution is to use Eucharistic Prayer D with its provision for intercessory petitions. These petitions, however, are prayers not so much of the *people* as of the *presider*. The people have no way to contribute to them.

Another solution is to use the general intercessions with two exchanges of peace, one before and one after. The first peace is a kiss or similar sign given only to the newly baptized; the second is a sign exchanged among all the people. This solution has the advantage of emphasizing the uniqueness of the newly baptized. They receive a special kiss of greeting as they enter the household of God, and then they exercise their priesthood by joining in the prayers of all the faithful and by exchanging the universal sign of reconciliation.

In *The Ceremonies of the Eucharist: A Guide to Celebration*, Howard Galley provides a litany for the prayers of the people at baptism or confirmation.[2]

Confirmation
BCP 412-419, BAS 623-630

When confirmation occurs separately from baptism, the prayer book allows the community to use the Prayers for the Candidates (BCP 417). These, however, are prayers for *baptismal* candidates, and it is better to omit them or to compose a more appropriate litany. The Canadian book provides a bidding litany for confirmation with phrases adapted from the litany for baptismal candidates (BAS 627-628).

At the end of the confirmations, receptions, and reaffirmations, the service continues "with the Prayers of the People or the Offertory of the Eucharist" (BCP 419). This rubric introduces a problem similar to the one in baptism. How can

---

2   Howard E. Galley, *The Ceremonies of the Eucharist: A Guide to Celebration* (Cambridge, Mass.: Cowley Publications, 1989), 231-232.

the assembly pray for those in need? To avoid any implication that confirmation and the other reaffirmation rites are the completion of baptism, it is desirable to have only one exchange of the peace, followed by the general intercessions. The peace cannot come after the intercessions without violating the order in the prayer book.

The Canadian confirmation liturgy simply omits the intercessions (BAS 629).[3]

Marriage
BCP 422-438, BAS 526-550

The *Book of Common Prayer* provides intercessions for the marriage liturgy (BCP 429). This is a series of petitions led by a deacon "or other person appointed." There are nine petitions, in a style resembling the prayer "for the whole state of Christ's Church" in Rite One. After each prayer the people respond, "Amen." A petition asking for children may be omitted, but there is no other provision for adapting or replacing the prayers.[4]

The community may use an alternative marriage rite, containing prayers "for the husband and wife, for their life together, for the Christian community, and for the world" (BCP 436). These rubrics allow them to borrow, adapt, or compose intercessions for the customary marriage rite.

The Canadian book gives a series of petitions based on the Episcopal ones, brief and simple in style. Each ends with "Lord, in your mercy" and the response "Hear our prayer" (BAS 532-533). These prayers are led "by a friend or a member of a family of the bride or groom, or by the celebrant or another minister."

For the blessing of a civil marriage, the prayer book makes the same provision for intercessions (BCP 434). The Canadian church provides three petitions for the prayers of the people (OC 60-61).

When a couple renew marriage vows, perhaps on their anniversary, it is appropriate to mention their names in the prayers of the people. Suitable leaders include a friend or member of the family (BOS 161, OC 57).

In a liturgy for the ending of a marriage, the Canadian prayer book suggests intercessions or thanksgivings for all those affected, including children, family and friends who are divided, and supporting friends. The liturgy includes several petitions and responses for this purpose (OC 66-72).

---

3   For a litany with a bidding for those who have been confirmed or received or who have renewed their baptismal vows, see Galley's *Ceremonies of the Eucharist*, 231-232.

4   For another litany for a marriage, see pages 123-124.

Birth or Adoption of a Child
BCP 439-445, BAS 610-614

The prayer book provides a liturgy for thanksgiving after a child has been born or adopted. When this occurs in the eucharist, it follows the prayers of the people. The leader or someone else should mention the child and parents by name. The *Book of Alternative Services* makes no special provision.

Ministry to the Sick
BCP 453-461, BAS 551-558

Ministry to the sick includes a liturgy that allows prayers "according to the occasion" (BCP 454, BAS 554). This provision occurs near the end of a liturgy of the word, the normal place for intercessions in a eucharistic liturgy. A collection of prayers for the sick appears on pages 458-460 of the *Book of Common Prayer*, and other sources provide many such prayers. Although the Canadian book does not provide prayers for the sick, many psalm prayers are appropriate. The prayers may be of any form and style—one or more collects or a litany—as long as they are intercessory.

The minister(s) of the liturgy, the sick person, and others who are present may pray for the sick person, his or her family, and the doctors, nurses, and others who are giving care. If possible, the sick person should have an opportunity to take part through responses and free prayer. Petitions for the cure of specific disorders are in order, but it is a superior sign of our union with Christ to pray for the health of the whole person and for the strength and patience to endure affliction.

The *Book of Occasional Services* provides a special Litany of Healing for public healing services (BOS 163-165). It consists of a Trinitarian invocation, a series of petitions addressed to God, and a concluding collect. At the beginning the people may name those for whom they are interceding.

Death and Burial
BCP 462-507, BAS 559-605

The liturgy for the dying and those who have died consists of a series of stations or pauses along the journey of death. At each stop we remember, give thanks, and pray for the dying or dead person and others.

The first station occurs when a person is near death. For the time of death, the prayer book provides a litany and other prayers (BCP 462–465, BAS 559–564). It is desirable that members of the family, friends, and, if possible, the dying person join in this liturgy. The litany is the most intercessory of the prayers, based on several medieval litanies. It begins with a Trinitarian address, includes a number of petitions and responses for specific needs, and concludes with the *Agnus Dei* and a triple *Kyrie*. Anyone may lead any part of this liturgy.

For this station the leader may use prayers in combination with the liturgy for the sick. The prayers may be said in three places:

(1) At the end of the liturgy of the word: the prayer for a person near death and the litany at the time of death;

(2) Just before communion: the Lord's Prayer and collect "Deliver your servant";

(3) In place of the postcommunion prayer and dismissal: the three commendatory prayers.

The *Book of Alternative Services* has similar prayers for commendation.

The second station is a vigil before the funeral. The prayer book provides a litany commending the dead person to God (BCP 465–466). Based on a litany from Gethsemani Abbey in Kentucky, it uses a response suggested by the last words of Christ: "Into your hands, O Lord, we commend our brother (sister) *N*." The litany at the time of death may be said instead. Anyone may lead these prayers.

For this station the Canadian book provides prayers for use in the dead person's home or elsewhere; there is no litany.

The third station is the funeral. The prayer book provides intercessions for both Rite One and Rite Two (BCP 480–481, 497). The Rite One intercessions are a series of ten collects (four may be omitted) suggesting the "whole state" prayer, with the people responding "Amen" after each. There is no provision for changes or substitutions, other than naming the dead person and adding the name of a saint. A deacon or someone else leads.

The Rite Two intercessions come from the burial rite of the Roman Catholic Church, a series of six short petitions (two may be omitted) with the people responding "Hear us, Lord." Since the litany alludes to "I am the resurrection and the life," Martha and Mary, and Lazarus, it is especially appropriate when the gospel reading is John 11:21–27. Anyone may lead the litany, but the presider says a concluding collect. The vigil litany or the Rite One prayers may be used instead.

The *Book of Common Prayer* allows the use of an alternative burial rite, containing prayers "for the deceased, for those who mourn, and for the Christian community, remembering the promises of God in Christ about eternal life" (BCP 506). These rubrics may also be used to compose intercessions in the normal burial rite, whether Rite One or Rite Two.[5]

The Canadian book gives one litany for both of its funeral liturgies. It consists of seven petitions led by a deacon or other member of the congregation, "appropriately a member of the family or a friend of the deceased person." After each petition the people respond, "Hear us, Lord." The book also suggests a time "for silent remembrance and thanksgiving" (BAS 579-580).

Ordination
BCP 510-555, BAS 631-665

In ordinations to all three orders, after the presentation the ordaining bishop calls on everybody to pray:

> All kneel, and the Person appointed leads the Litany for Ordinations, or some other approved litany. (BCP 515, 527, 539)

In some places those to be ordained prostrate themselves on the floor, a position considered an ancient form of kneeling. The leader may be a deacon or anyone else; often it is someone who can chant the litany well. After the litany the bishop stands and then sings or says the salutation and collect.

The Litany for Ordinations (BCP 548-551) is solemn, long, and hard on arthritic knees. It starts with Trinitarian invocations and ends with a triple *Kyrie*. Based on Form V of the prayers of the people, the body of the litany covers in sixteen biddings many needs of the church and the world. Four biddings ask prayer for the ordinands and their families, household members, or communities. The final commendation may include remembrance of "the ever-blessed Virgin Mary" and other saints.

But what is "some other approved litany" allowed by the rubrics? Presumably it is any other litany the bishop approves for use at that ordination. Some places use a version of the traditional litany of the saints. Any litany, chosen or composed, should include prayers for the ordinands and should adequately cover the needs of the church and the world.

---

5   For another litany for a burial, see pages 124-125.

The Canadian book places the ordination litany immediately before the hymn *Veni Creator Spiritus* (or *Veni Sancte Spiritus*) and provides two forms of the litany (BAS 661-664). The first is similar to the Episcopal litany but shorter, omitting four biddings. The second opens with Trinitarian invocations, contains twelve brief petitions based on medieval and other sources, and ends with the *Trisagion* and a collect.

Celebration of a New Ministry
BCP 557-565, OC 82-98

The intercessions in the Episcopal liturgy for a celebration of a new ministry are similar to those for ordination. Near the beginning, after the institution ceremony, "the Litany for Ordinations, or some other appropriate litany, is led by a person appointed." The litany is sung or said standing or kneeling, and the bishop, if present, stands for the salutation and collect at the end.

The intercessions in the Canadian liturgy come in two forms. In the first, before the peace "members of the community may lead the congregation in prayers for the Church, for the world, and for all people." The second provides that prayers of the people "may be led by a number of members of the congregation." The form prints four biddings and suggests others "for the world, the Church, the local community, the sick, friends and family of those present, and the departed." The leaders end each bidding with "Lord, in your mercy," and the people respond "Hear our prayer."

Consecration of a Church
BCP 566-579, OC 126-143

In the Episcopal liturgy for the consecration of a church, the general intercessions occur in the normal place, after the sermon (and Nicene Creed). A deacon "or a member of the congregation" leads the prayers. No form is given, but the prayer book allows free use of local creativity:

> Any of the usual forms of the Prayers of the People may be used; or some other
> form may be composed for the occasion, having due regard for the distinctive
> nature of the community, and with commemoration of benefactors, donors,
> artists, artisans, and others. (BCP 576)

The intercessions of the eucharist are not to be confused with the Litany of Thanksgiving for a Church (BCP 578-579), which is suggested for occasions such as the patronal feast or the anniversary of dedication or consecration. When used, this thanksgiving probably should come either after the intercessions, before the eucharistic prayer, or before the dismissal (replacing the postcommunion prayer and blessing).

The Canadian blessing of a church or chapel does not provide for prayers of the people (see comments, OC 128).

Other Special Liturgies

Dedication of Church Furnishings and Ornaments *(BOS 192-209)*
Normally the dedication of furnishings and ornaments follows the sermon (and creed) at the eucharist. The prayers of the people may be omitted. If they are used, they may contain remembrance of benefactors and persons to be commemorated. The Canadian church does not provide for blessing church objects.

Founding of a Church *(BOS 210-216)*
Consisting mainly of groundbreaking, the liturgy begins with a procession to the site of the building. A Litany for the Church (Trinitarian invocations, seven "O Christ" petitions, and other petitions) is sung or said during the procession.

Reaffirmation of Ordination Vows *(BOS 231-234)*
This liturgy often takes place on Maundy Thursday or earlier in Holy Week, at clergy conferences, and at meetings of the presbyters and/or deacons of a diocese. The prayers of the people may be omitted in this liturgy (BOS 229). If they are used, the intercessions should name the bishop and refer specifically to the presbyters and deacons.

If chrism is consecrated at the same liturgy, or at any other liturgy apart from baptism, intercessions should include those preparing for baptism. Similarly, if oil of the sick is blessed, the prayers of the people should mention those to be anointed and all the sick.

Welcoming New People to a Congregation *(BOS 110, OC 45)*
Although the Episcopal directions do not mention intercession, the prayers may include the names of new people. The Canadian book provides petitions for this purpose.

When Members Leave a Congregation *(BOS 111, OC 47)*
Although the Episcopal directions do not mention intercession, the prayers may include the names of departing members. The Canadian book provides petitions for this purpose.

Celebration for a Home *(BOS 142-152, OC 149-158)*
In the Episcopal Church, prayers during a procession through the house replace the prayers of the people. In the Canadian church, if the home is new, there is a similar procession; if the home is established, the worshipers stay in a central room and use a litany of intercession (several are suggested).

Various Blessings
The *Book of Occasional Services* and *Occasional Celebrations* contain many other rites of blessing on special occasions. In most of these it is appropriate to mention in the prayers of the people the persons or objects being blessed.

Part III

℘

Resources

8

Categories of Intercession

Those who plan intercessions for public use in church, as well as those who practice intercessory prayer in private, will find it helpful to remember that all intercessory prayer covers two main categories, the *church* and the *world*. Both the *Book of Common Prayer* (BCP 359, 383) and the *Book of Alternative Services* (BAS 53, 70, 190) encourage us to divide these two categories into six parts when we plan intercessory prayers:

1. The church
2. The nation and all in authority
3. The world
4. The community
5. The needy
6. The dead.

These six parts form the basis for the lists of topics described in this chapter. Scattered among the topics are comments, biddings, and sample petitions to be used as guides. Over an extended period, such as a year, intercessory prayer should cover most of the topics listed, but it is not usually desirable to use the entire list on any one occasion. A few topics should be selected that are appropriate for this time, this place, this person, this congregation.

1. The Church

First we remember the church. Even if we do not go into detail about the bishop and other leaders, we offer the church to God. It may seem strange to offer the body of Christ to God, but the body in all its glory is also a congregation of quarreling sinners who struggle to find their way on a difficult journey. Of all enterprises the assembled body must contend the hardest to reproduce the divine image, and thus of all human activities the body most needs our prayers.

The concept *church* comes from Hebrew and Greek words meaning *gathering* or *assembly*. To pray for the church is to pray for the welfare of the gathered people of God. To pray for the church is to remember its mission to proclaim the good news, its leaders and others who minister, and all its members.

One, holy, catholic, and apostolic church in every place

> Let us pray for the holy Catholic Church of Christ throughout the world…that God will confirm his Church in faith, increase it in love, and preserve it in peace.
>
> *Liturgy of Good Friday*

Mission of the church

> Let us pray for the spread of God's reign in every place, and for those who go forth bearing the good news.

> O God, you have made of one blood all the peoples of the earth, and sent your blessed Son to preach peace to those who are far off and to those who are near: Grant that people everywhere may seek after you and find you; bring the nations into your fold; pour out your Spirit upon all flesh; and hasten the coming of your kingdom; through Jesus Christ our Lord.
>
> *BCP, Morning Prayer*

Archbishop of Canterbury

Descended from a long line of archbishops beginning with the Benedictine monk Augustine, who came to England from Rome in 597, the archbishop of Canterbury is the titular leader of all Anglicans. Although the archbishop does not exercise jurisdiction outside England, the Anglican leader exercises a profound spiritual influence as first among equals and as a sign of unity. In praying for the archbishop of Canterbury, we are united with other Anglicans throughout the world.

> Let us pray for *N.* of Canterbury, first among equals in the churches of the Anglican communion.

The pope
The ecumenical patriarch
Leaders of other churches
In this ecumenical age, many branches of the church are seeking to recover the unity they once had. Through consultations and discussions, common worship, and common acts of ministry in the world, many Christians are working toward the goal of worldwide communion. The principal figure of all the churches is the Roman Catholic pope. In the Eastern Orthodox churches, the patriarch of Constantinople, or ecumenical patriarch, occupies a position similar to that of the archbishop of Canterbury for Anglicans.

Prayer for ecumenism occurs during the Week of Prayer for Christian Unity, January 18-25 (from the Confession of Saint Peter through the Conversion of Saint Paul). We should remember not only the leaders of other churches but also the ecumenical discussions among Anglicans and Roman Catholics, Eastern Orthodox, Lutherans, and others.

> Let us pray for the leaders of all the churches, especially the pope and the patriarch of Constantinople.

> Let us pray for the welfare and unity of all the churches.

Our presiding bishop and primate
Each church in the Anglican Communion has a primate, or chief bishop. Each church decides the title, jurisdiction, and functions of its primate. Most primates are called "archbishop," but there are a few exceptions, including the "primus" of the Scottish Episcopal Church and the "presiding bishop" of the American church (who presides over the House of Bishops). Some primates are also diocesan bishops. The Episcopal primate, who has no diocese, spends much of his time traveling throughout this vast church, visiting, and ordaining new bishops.

> Let us pray for our presiding bishop, primate of the Episcopal Church.

Our diocese and this congregation

The local church is the gathering of the people of God, where worship and ministry take place, and from which the people go forth to love and serve the Lord. As used by Anglicans, the term "local church" means both the diocese (which in the early church was a congregation) and the congregation. Each local church represents all Christian life; it is not merely a branch of a national or worldwide church. The universal or catholic church is formed in the local churches, and it exists out of them, as a communion of them.

> Let us pray for our diocese and all its people, and for our congregation and all its people.

> Let us pray for all the holy people of God and for our leaders, the bishops who preside in dioceses and the presbyters who preside in congregations.

Our bishop and every bishop

We pray for bishops because they stand for the unity, catholicity, and apostolicity of the church. By standing for these sacred characteristics, the bishops help to bring them about, both within their diocese and throughout the church. Bishops preside over the sacramental life in dioceses, guard and teach the faith delivered by Christ, and join with other bishops in a college or household.

> Let us pray for N. our bishop, and for all the bishops of the holy catholic church throughout the world.

Anglican cycle of prayer

The Anglican cycle of prayer is a calendar of intercessions for every Anglican bishop and diocese. It is used throughout the Anglican Communion, and is distributed in the United States by Forward Movement Publications.

> Let us pray for all the bishops and dioceses of the Anglican Communion, especially for N.

Diocesan cycle of prayer

Each diocese has a calendar of intercessions for every congregation (parish, mission, chapel). This usually lists the priests and deacons (and sometimes their spouses) by name. It is designed for use throughout the diocese.

> Let us pray for the congregations of our diocese, for their priests and deacons, and for other ministries of the diocese, especially N.

Our presider and all presbyters

After the bishop, the person most needing our daily prayers is the priest who presides in our congregation. Every presider is the deputy of the bishop in this place.

> Let us pray for *N*. our presbyter(s) and for all presbyters.

Deacons and all who minister in Christ

In many dioceses deacons are a common sight, and some congregations have two or more. The primary role of deacons in the modern church is to lead Christians in the care of those in need. But other roles are also important. Some deacons work in diocesan administration, which was the main role of deacons in the early church. All deacons are agents of the bishop and members of the bishop's household or staff.

> Let us pray for *N*. our deacon(s), for all deacons, and for all who minister in our congregation.

Readers and cantors and all who proclaim the word

Readers appear on the lists of martyrs in the early church. In an age when literacy was not as widespread as it is today, they were appointed for life and served with great distinction. Almost as valuable were the cantors or psalmists, who chanted the gradual (the psalm sung from the *gradus* or step below the ambo) and other psalms and liturgical texts.

In the twentieth century, the church has restored the ancient and venerable ministry of reader, but without requiring an official appointment. In many places the church has also revived the ministry of cantor or song leader, those who sing the gradual psalm and lead the people in their singing.

Readers (or lectors) are different from licensed lay readers, whose ministry is mainly to lead public worship. They also need our prayers.

> Let us pray for all who proclaim the word of God in the Christian assembly,
> by reading the holy scriptures and by singing psalms and other songs.

Preachers who speak the word of truth

In the words of the *Book of Common Prayer* and the *Book of Alternative Services*, it is "the bishop's prerogative" to preach in the eucharistic liturgy. Thus, the normative preacher in every congregation is the bishop; in the bishop's absence, it is the priest. The usual preacher (the one we usually have) is the priest. There are exceptions to this rule. Assisting priests, visiting priests, deacons, dignitaries, and licensed preachers sometimes preach. We pray that God will cleanse their hearts and lips and speak the truth through their mouths.

Let us pray for all who preach.

Those who bring the eucharist to absent members

From 1952 through 1970, the Episcopal Church ordained "perpetual" deacons to help in administering the sacrament, and in taking it to the sick and shut-in. In the last two decades the church has licensed "eucharistic ministers" to do this job. It is now common for these ministers to serve the chalice, and sometimes the bread, at the altar rail. In many places they also take the body and blood of Christ directly from the altar to communicants who could not be present. Those who extend the eucharist in this manner help the assembly to become complete.

Let us pray for eucharistic ministers.

Those who lead and serve the assembly at prayer

These include ushers, acolytes, sacristans, the altar guild, musicians, the liturgy committee, and all others concerned with worship and the public prayer of the community.

Let us pray for all the other liturgical ministers of the Christian gathering.

All who minister

Ministry is an assigned task to carry out the will of God. Those who minister, whether ordained or not ordained, are intermediaries in word and deed, agents, messengers, and personal attendants. They bear the authority of those who send them.

> Almighty and everlasting God, by whose Spirit the whole body of your faithful people is governed and sanctified: Receive our supplications and prayers which we offer before you for all members of your holy Church, that in their vocation and ministry they may truly and devoutly serve you; through our Lord and Savior Jesus Christ.
>
> *BCP, Morning Prayer*

Catechumens seeking life in Christ

Catechumens are unbaptized adults seeking life in Christ, and the catechumenate is a period of preparation for their baptism. In the early church, when many adults sought baptism, this period was an important part of the liturgical life in each community. In an age when the world is again increasingly pagan and many adults grow up ignorant of the Christian life, the modern church has revived the catechumenate. Prayers for catechumens are especially appropriate during Lent, the season when adults throughout the church are completing their preparation for baptism at the Easter Vigil.

> Let us pray for the catechumens and their formation as Christians.

Catechists and sponsors

Catechumens become Christians by entering into the life of a Christian community. In this process the most important members of that community are those who take the catechumens by the hand and lead them.

> Let us pray for those who lead the catechumens to their baptism at the Great Vigil of Easter.

Newly baptized brothers and sisters

Prayers for the newly baptized are especially appropriate during the fifty days of Easter. In the ancient church this period was called *mystagogy*, or initiation into the mysteries. As neophytes experience the sacraments of the church, they become more firmly bound into the community of Christians.

> Let us pray for those who are newly baptized in Christ, who gives living water to all who thirst.

> Almighty God, by the Passover of your Son you have brought us out of sin into righteousness and out of death into life: Grant to those who are sealed by your Holy Spirit the will and the power to proclaim you to all the world; through Jesus Christ our Lord.
>
> *BCP, Easter Vigil*

All the baptized

> Let us pray for all baptized Christians, for God has anointed their head with oil, clothed them in Christ, and spread a table before them.

Almighty and everlasting God, who in the Paschal mystery established the new covenant of reconciliation: Grant that all who are reborn into the fellowship of Christ's Body may show forth in their lives what they profess by their faith; through Jesus Christ our Lord.

BCP, Easter Vigil

Those who renew their baptismal vows

Alongside the catechumenate exists a formation process for baptized adults who are seeking reaffirmation of vows and renewal of their life in Christ. This also is a process in which the entire Christian community participates through prayer and support.

Let us pray for those who renew their baptismal vows in the communion of the church.

Evangelists and all who bear the gospel
Prophets and all who speak the truth
Teachers and mentors in the holy way
Spiritual directors, guides, and companions
Monks, nuns, friars, hermits, and anchorites
Those who offer their gifts to God

Alongside the elected and appointed ministers of the church are those with special gifts:

The gifts [Christ] gave were that some would be apostles, some prophets, some evangelists, some pastors and teachers. (Ephesians 4:11)

One emphasis of our age has been a return to spiritual discipline. The spiritual life requires counseling by directors and other guides, and many seek guidance and inspiration from those who live under a monastic rule.

Let us pray for those with special gifts, and for those who guide us in the spiritual life.

Those who give food to the hungry
Those who give drink to the thirsty
Those who welcome the stranger
Those who give clothing to the naked
Those who care for the sick

Those who visit the prisoners
Those who comfort the dying and bury the dead
The account of the great judgment of Christ (Matthew 25:31-46) shows that all who care for those in need encounter Christ in the act of caring. In the middle ages burying the dead was added to this list of six categories, to become the Seven Corporal Works of Mercy.

Let us pray for those who care for the needy.

Those who bring light into the world
Those who challenge others with the gospel
Those who teach and guide
Those who heal and care and counsel
Those who listen and encourage
Those who bear wrongs and forgive injuries
Those who pray for the living and the dead
In addition to the Seven Corporal Works of Mercy, there are Seven Spiritual Works of Mercy, as traditionally listed in the middle ages. Today we may sum them up as works of holy listening, counseling, and prayer for others. Spiritual works often take place at the same time and in the same milieu as corporal works.

Let us pray for those who convert, teach, counsel, comfort, endure, forgive, and pray.

God of all wisdom and knowledge, give your blessing and guidance to all who teach, that by word and example they may lead those whom they teach to the knowledge and love of you; through Jesus Christ our Lord.
BOS, Commissioning for Lay Ministries

Those who work for justice, mercy, and peace
In the modern church Christians are interested in Social Works of Mercy, developing a list that is more corporate and widespread than the older corporal and spiritual works.

All persons in their vocations

Let us offer prayers to God who bestows gifts on all the holy people.

O Lord, without whom our labor is lost: We beseech you to prosper all works in your Church undertaken according to your holy will. Grant to your workers a pure intention, a patient faith, sufficient success on earth, and the blessedness of serving you in heaven; through Jesus Christ our Lord.

BOS, Commissioning for Lay Ministries

Those celebrating baptismal days
One consequence of the recovery of baptism as the primary sacrament is the keepsing of one's "baptismal day," the anniversary of one's baptism. Just as we remember our birthday, we should know our baptismal day, and we should also know the baptismal days of others. Many congregations pray for those with baptismal days during the coming week.

Those celebrating wedding anniversaries
The anniversary of marriage vows also needs our prayers in the community eucharist. This remembrance helps the congregation to understand Christ's love and the living signs of unity in our midst.

God of the covenant, hear our prayer, and accept all we offer you this day. You have made *N.* and *N.* one in the sacrament of marriage. May the mystery of Christ's unselfish love increase their love for you and for each other; through Christ our Lord.

BAS, Marriage

Those preparing for ordination (Ember Day I)
Four times a year, roughly at the beginning of each new season, the Ember Days provide occasions for praying for those whom the people of God have chosen for ordained ministry.

Let us offer prayers to God who chooses bishops, priests, and deacons by the action of the body of Christ.

Everliving God, strengthen and sustain those who are to be ordained, that with patience and understanding they may love and care for your people; and grant that together they may follow Jesus Christ, offering to you their gifts and talents; through him who lives and reigns with you and the Holy Spirit, one God, for ever and ever.

BCP, Celebration of a New Ministry, adapted

The selection of persons for ordination (Ember Day II)

Let us offer prayers to God who creates order in the gathered people.

O God, you led your holy apostles to ordain ministers in every place: Grant that your Church, under the guidance of the Holy Spirit, may choose suitable persons for the ministry of Word and Sacrament, and may uphold them in their work for the extension of your kingdom; through Jesus Christ our Lord.
BCP, Collect for the choice of fit persons for the ministry

Church buildings and other holy places

Although "church" refers primarily to an assembly of holy people, from early times the buildings in which they gather have also gained an aura of holiness. Especially on the patronal feast of a parish, or on the anniversary of the consecration of its building, we pray for this place.

Let us offer prayers to God who gathers us in this house of the Lord.

Almighty God, all times are your seasons, and all occasions invite your tender mercies: Accept our prayers and intercessions offered in this place today and in the days to come; through Jesus Christ, our Mediator and Advocate.
BCP, Consecration of a Church

Church conventions

At the time of the annual convention, we pray for the bishop and delegates who gather to worship and conduct the business of the diocese.

Let us offer prayers to God who accepts the words of our mouth and the meditation of our heart.

Source of all wisdom and understanding, be present with those who take counsel [*in this place*] for the renewal and mission of your Church. Teach us in all things to seek first your honor and glory. Guide us to perceive what is right, and grant us both the courage to pursue it and the grace to accomplish it; through Jesus Christ our Lord.
BCP, Prayer 12, For a Church Convention or Meeting, adapted

The unity of the church

Above all, when we pray for the holy catholic church we beseech God to reveal its unity. Its division into sects and denominations, its quarrels and schisms, its neglect of hospitality at the holy table—all these are errors to be corrected. The ultimate unity of the body of Christ comes from the mystery of the Trinity, three persons in one God.

Let us offer prayers to God who calls us to stand within the gates of Jerusalem.

Gracious Father, we pray for your holy Catholic Church. Fill it with all truth, in all truth with all peace. Where it is corrupt, purify it; where it is in error, direct it; where in any thing it is amiss, reform it. Where it is right, strengthen it; where it is in want, provide for it; where it is divided, reunite it; for the sake of Jesus Christ your Son our Savior.

BCP, Prayer 7, For the Church

For you tend the vine of those who abide in you, and we give you glory, Father, Son, and Holy Spirit, for ever and ever.

O God of unchangeable power and eternal light, look favorably on your whole church, that wonderful and sacred mystery. By the effectual working of your providence, carry out in tranquility the plan of salvation. Let the whole world see and know that things which were cast down are being raised up, and things which had grown old are being made new, and that all things are being brought to their perfection by him through whom all things were made, your Son Jesus Christ our Lord, who lives and reigns with you, in the unity of the Holy Spirit, one God, for ever and ever.

Easter Vigil, from the Gelasian sacramentary (eighth century)

2. The Nation and All in Authority

Although earthly nations are no more than flickering shadows of the holy city Jerusalem, they share in the sacredness of God's creation. We pray for nations and other social and political groups and for their leaders, that the vision of the holy city may spread among all peoples and that mercy, justice, and peace may prevail in every place.

This nation
Prayers for the United States of America are especially appropriate on the Fourth of July, and prayers for Canada occur on July 1. Other nations also celebrate national holidays of liberation. Prayers for the nation should be frequent, however, occurring at least every Sunday.

Lord God Almighty, in whose Name the founders of this country won liberty for themselves and for us, and lit the torch of freedom for nations then unborn: Grant that we and all the people of this land may have grace to maintain our liberties in righteousness and peace; through Jesus Christ our Lord.

BCP, Independence Day

Our president, governor, and mayor
Our senators and representatives
Our state legislators
Our council members
Those running for public office
Those who protect our lives and property
Those in the armed forces
Former members of the armed forces
Police, deputies, and all law officers
Judges and courts of justice

We pray for the leaders of the nations and all in civil authority, "so that we may lead a quiet and peaceable life in all godliness and dignity" (1 Timothy 2:2). Those who govern and protect us are in constant peril from corruption and physical danger, and thus we too are in peril. We pray for them especially on days of civic importance and on election days.

3. The World

Every language, nation, and people on earth
Every tribe, clan, and family
Every city and place
The whole human family

Our idea of groups of people has widened beyond the nation state to include those who speak a language or dialect, those who belong to a tribe or clan or family in the largest sense. All these groups are engaged in a struggle to define their identity, to retain their valuable traditions, and to evolve and change as they adapt to modern circumstances.

Almighty God, whose wisdom and whose love are over all, accept the prayers we offer for every nation and people. Give integrity to all citizens and wisdom to those in authority, that harmony and justice may be secured in obedience to your will; through Jesus Christ our Lord.

BAS, Canada Day, alt.

In the following prayer for Africa, simply substitute the appropriate nation or people.

God bless Africa, guard her children, guide her leaders, and give her peace, for Jesus Christ's sake.

Good weather

When we pray for good weather, we ask not so much for sunshine on the weekend as for seasonable weather typical of the region, weather that will promote the growth of plants and animals, sustain human beings in health and safety, and cleanse the earth and atmosphere.

Let us offer prayers to God who prepares rain for the earth.

O gracious Father, who opens your hand and fills all things living with plenteousness: Bless the lands and waters, and multiply the harvests of the world; let your Spirit go forth, that it may renew the face of the earth; show your loving-kindness, that our land may give her increase; and save us from selfish use of what you give, that men and women everywhere may give you thanks; through Christ our Lord.

BCP, Prayer 42, For the Harvest of Lands and Waters

Abundant fruits of the earth

The traditional time for praying for fruitful seasons is the Rogation Days, on the Monday, Tuesday, and Wednesday before Ascension Day. In much of the northern hemisphere, at least, by this time we begin to see the results of spring planting.

Almighty God, we thank you for making the fruitful earth produce what is needed for life. Bless those who work in the fields; give us favorable weather; and grant that all may share the fruits of the earth, rejoicing in your goodness; through your Son Jesus Christ our Lord.

BAS, Occasional Prayers 19

For you make the grass to grow upon the mountains, and we give you glory, Father, Son, and Holy Spirit, for ever and ever.

Care of God's creation
Harvest of lands and waters

We pray for ourselves and for all those whose responsibility it is to care for the earth and air and water, for all that grows, and for all things formed on earth and throughout space. In the United States, Thanksgiving Day is the traditional time to give thanks for a fruitful harvest; prayers for a good harvest should occur during the summer.

> As we recall our stewardship of creation, let us offer prayers to God who provides for all the world.

> Creator of the fruitful earth, you made us stewards of all things. Give us grateful hearts for all your goodness, and steadfast wills to use your bounty well, that the whole human family, today and in generations to come, may with us give thanks for the riches of your creation. We ask this in the name of Jesus Christ our Lord.
>
> *BAS, Rogation Days, adapted*

> For you are clothed with majesty and splendor, and we give you glory, Father, Son, and Holy Spirit, for ever and ever.

Health and protection of the environment

> Almighty God our heavenly Father, you declare your glory and show forth your handiwork in the heavens and in the earth: Deliver us in our various occupations from the service of self alone, that we may do the work you give us to do in truth and beauty and for the common good; for the sake of him who came among us as one who serves, your Son Jesus Christ our Lord.
>
> *BCP, Collect for Vocation in Daily Work*

> For you satisfy the thirsty and fill the hungry with good things, and we give you glory, Father, Son, and Holy Spirit, for ever and ever.

Those who care for our environment

> Source of all life, heaven and earth are yours, yet you have given us dominion over all things. Receive the prayers we offer you this day, in the name of Jesus Christ our Lord.
>
> *BAS, Rogation Days, adapted*

Animals who do our work, help to feed us, and keep us company
All God's creatures under heaven
The customary time for praying for animals (and blessing them) is the feast day of Saint Francis of Assisi (October 4) or the Sunday after that. These should include not merely household pets but domestic animals and wildlife of all kinds.

Peace
Peace among the nations
Those who work for peace
All who keep the peace
The incessant prayer of all human beings is for peace—peace among nations, religions, regions, families, gangs, people. Peace that brings no more war and no more violence, peace in deliverance from all our affliction, strife, and need. Peace that is the breath of God blowing across all creation. *Shalom, salaam,* peace. Because it is such a universal desire, every time of prayer should include a petition for peace.

> Eternal God, in whose perfect kingdom no sword is drawn but the sword of righteousness, no strength known but the strength of love: So mightily spread abroad your Spirit, that all peoples may be gathered under the banner of the Prince of Peace, as children of one Father; to whom be dominion and glory, now and for ever.
>
> *BCP, Prayer 4, For Peace*

> O God, it is your will to hold both heaven and earth in a single peace. Let the design of your great love shine on the waste of our wraths and sorrows, and give peace to your Church, peace among nations, peace in our homes, and peace in our hearts; through your Son Jesus Christ our Lord.
>
> *BAS, Occasional Prayers 6*

> For you speak peace to your faithful people, and we give you glory, Father, Son, and Holy Spirit, for ever and ever.

4. The Community

We have already prayed for the leaders of the community and for all who govern, judge, and keep order. Now it is time to pray for the concerns and needs of the communities in which we live and work.

We pray for this city [town, place] and those who live here.

O Lord our creator, by your holy prophet you taught your ancient people to seek the welfare of the cities in which they lived. We commend our neighbourhood [city, town, village, community] to your care, that it might be kept free from social strife and decay. Give us strength of purpose and concern for others, that we may create here a community of justice and peace where your will may be done; through Jesus Christ our Lord.

BAS, For the Neighbourhood, adapted

5. The Needy

The largest category of intercessions includes all those in danger and need; the sick and the suffering; prisoners, captives, and their families; the hungry, homeless, and oppressed; all those in situations of change, uncertainty, and crisis. Although intercession is normally prayer for others, here we also pray for ourselves, for our well-being affects the well-being of our families, friends, and neighbors.

Those preparing for marriage
All married couples
All those who live in covenanted relationships
All households and families
When we pray for families, we offer prayers to God who made the holy people one flesh in marvelous diversity. The term "family" needs to be interpreted in a broad sense, including not only husbands and wives and their children, but also all those related by blood and marriage, and those who live in communities of friends and neighbors. In many places the term has extended to include those of the same sex living together in a covenant of love.

Eternal God, creator and preserver of all life, author of salvation, and giver of all grace: Look with favor upon the world you have made, and for which your Son gave his life, and especially upon this man and this woman whom you make one flesh in Holy Matrimony.

BCP, Marriage

O God, whose desire is that all the peoples of the world should be one human family, living together in harmony, grant that our home [family, union], by its worship and its witness, may help to hasten the day when your will is done on earth as it is in heaven; through Jesus Christ our Lord.

BAS, For Home and Family, adapted

Women bearing children and all mothers
Unmarried parents
Mothers and fathers who have lost their children
Children who have died through abortion and miscarriage
Orphans and abandoned children
Infants, children, and all young people

The dangers of childbirth have not entirely disappeared but have been supplemented by a host of new perils, especially to children.

Travelers
Those at risk on land, on water, and in the air
Those at risk underwater and underground
Explorers and workers in outer space

The travels of Paul by land and sea show how dangerous such journeys were in the ancient world. They still are dangerous, and we still need to pray for those who have set out from the relative safety of home for a long and often risky trip. We now also travel in the air, in outer space, and under the water, at even greater risk.

All persons in their daily work
Those who work in agriculture
Those who work in industry
Those whose work is difficult and dangerous
Those who work at home

> Almighty God, whose Son Jesus Christ in his earthly life shared our toil and hallowed our labor: Be present with your people where they work; make those who carry on the industries and commerce of this land responsive to your will; and give to us all a pride in what we do, and a just return for our labor; through Jesus Christ our Lord.
>
> *BCP, Collect for Rogation Days II*

> O God, in the course of this busy life, give us times of refreshment and peace; and grant that we may so use our leisure to rebuild our bodies and renew

our minds, that our spirits may be opened to the goodness of your creation; through Jesus Christ our Lord.

BCP, Prayer 32, For the Good Use of Leisure

The poor and needy
Those who have suffered economic failure
Those who are unemployed and destitute
All who suffer because of technology and competition
Widows and widowers
Those who are elderly and lonely
Those who are separated and divorced
Those who have attempted suicide
The frightened and threatened
Those who are hungry and thirsty
Those who are naked and homeless

The ancient scriptural categories of persons at risk included widows, orphans, and aliens (or strangers). The common element was loneliness, being without the support of family and tribe. Adjusting the categories to apply to modern conditions, we find that loneliness still puts us at risk—economic, social, physical, emotional, and spiritual. Thus, we become subject to hunger and homelessness.

Those suffering from sickness

The greatest loneliness of all comes to us in sickness, in which we lose touch with ourselves, with others, and with God.

Let us offer prayers to God who heals the sick and forgives sins.

O God, the strength of the weak and the comfort of sufferers: Mercifully accept our prayers, and grant to those who are sick the help of your power, that their sickness may be turned into health, and our sorrow into joy; through Jesus Christ our Lord.

BCP, Ministration to the Sick, adapted

O God of heavenly powers, by the might of your command you drive away from our bodies all sickness and all infirmity: Be present in your goodness with those who are sick, that their weakness may be banished and their strength restored; and that, their health being renewed, they may bless your holy Name; through Jesus Christ our Lord.

BCP, Ministration to the Sick, adapted

Those who are HIV-positive and those suffering from AIDS
Those suffering from disabling and chronic diseases
Alcoholics and other abusers of drugs
The deaf and the blind
Those who are paralyzed or disabled
Those who are hindered and disadvantaged
The mentally ill and emotionally disturbed
Victims of famine, drought, and pollution
All victims of social injustice

Many of those in need are victims of some natural or human-made disaster. Just as we pray for peace, for mercy and justice, and for good weather, we pray for those whose condition results from the absence of those merciful conditions.

Let us offer prayers to God, who has pity on the lowly and poor.

Grant, O God, that your holy and life-giving Spirit may so move every human heart and especially the hearts of the people of this land, that barriers which divide us may crumble, suspicions disappear, and hatreds cease; that our divisions being healed, we may live in justice and peace; through Jesus Christ our Lord.

BCP, Prayer 27, For Social Justice

Look with pity, O heavenly Father, upon the people in this land who live with injustice, terror, disease, and death as their constant companions. Have mercy upon us. Help us to eliminate our cruelty to these our neighbors. Strengthen those who spend their lives establishing equal protection of the law and equal opportunities for all. And grant that every one of us may enjoy a fair portion of the riches of this land; through Jesus Christ our Lord.

BCP, Prayer 36, For the Oppressed

Prisoners and captives and their families
Those on death row
Former inmates on the outside
Refugees and exiles
Hostages and their families
Political prisoners and detainees

Since ancient times Christians have prayed for those in prison and other captivity. Today the category of captives has expanded. We are concerned not merely for those whose imprisonment involves the wreckage of lives. We pray also for those under sentence of death, hostages, and those released from prison who are trying to resume normal lives. Since we recognize that imprisonment affects a wide circle of persons, we pray also for their families.

> Lord Jesus, who for our sake was condemned as a criminal, visit our jails and prisons with your pity and judgment. Remember all prisoners and comfort their families. Remember those who work in these institutions and give them compassion. And since what we do for those in prison, O Lord, we do for you, help us to improve their lot. All this we ask for your mercy's sake.
>
> *BCP, Prayer 37, For Prisons and Correctional Institutions, adapted*

Aliens, migrants, and strangers
Indigenous peoples of the world
Those who have no home

Another ancient category of prayer is the one who is away from home, the alien or stranger.

> Merciful God, we remember before you all those who are aliens, migrants, and strangers in this world, those who wander in the streets, and those who have no home. Heal them in body and spirit and turn their loneliness into joy; through Jesus Christ our Lord.
>
> *Based on BAS, For the Poor and Neglected*

Those who suffer the effects of war, oppression, and strife
Victims of robbery, violence, and rape
Those in slavery and bitter servitude
Those who suffer from discrimination in race, age, and sex
Abused women, men, and children
Those in broken families
Children in need of care and love

We pray especially for those at risk from war, violence, and civil and social disorder.

> Look with pity, O heavenly Father, on those who live in peril from war, violence, and disorder. Have mercy on them in their weakness and vulnerability, and help us to eliminate injustice, terror, and cruelty wherever they are found; through Jesus Christ our Lord.
>
> *Based on BAS, For the Oppressed in this Land*

Those who hate us and those who persecute us
Our enemies
Those who do not believe in God or know the love of God
Those who have wandered from the way
Christians are to pray for their enemies, for those who have left the faith, and for those who do not believe in God.

> O God, the Father of all, whose Son commanded us to love our enemies: Lead them and us from prejudice to truth; deliver them and us from hatred, cruelty, and revenge; and in your good time enable us all to stand reconciled before you; through Jesus Christ our Lord.
>
> *BCP, Prayer 6, For our Enemies*

> Merciful God, Creator of all the peoples of the earth and lover of souls: Have compassion on all who do not know you as you are revealed in your Son Jesus Christ; let your Gospel be preached with grace and power to those who have not heard it; turn the hearts of those who resist it; and bring home to your fold those who have gone astray; that there may be one flock under one shepherd, Jesus Christ our Lord.
>
> *BCP, Liturgy of Good Friday*

Jews, Muslims, and other believers
Christians also pray for those of other faiths, especially Jews and Muslims, and for all who seek the Divine.

> Blessed are you, God of all peoples, who calls all nations, tribes, clans, and families to be a holy people. In ancient times you summoned Abraham, Mohammed, and other holy leaders into covenant with you. Now gather under your wings people of faith throughout the world. Guard them in their journey, and guide them as they seek you, the Unity of Being and one true God. This we pray through Jesus Christ.

Sinners and penitents
We pray for those who sin and for those who are doing acts of penitence for their sins.

> Holy God, heavenly Father, you formed me from the dust in your image and likeness, and redeemed me from sin and death by the cross of your Son Jesus Christ. Through the water of baptism you clothed me with the shining

garment of his righteousness, and established me among your children in your kingdom. But I have squandered the inheritance of your saints, and have wandered far in a land that is waste.

BCP, The Reconciliation of a Penitent: Form II

Ourselves and one another
Forgiveness of our sins
Our deliverance from all affliction, strife, and need

Finally, among categories of the living, we pray for ourselves, for forgiveness, and for our safety.

For ourselves; for the forgiveness of our sins, and for the grace of the Holy Spirit to amend our lives, we pray to you, O Lord.

BCP, Prayers of the People, Form V

6. The Dead

Although death acquires its central meaning from the resurrection of Christ, it retains an ancient metaphor from both pagan and early Christian burial practices. In death one sets out on a journey, especially across a body of water. We give a dying person food for the journey (the bread and wine of the eucharist). Finally, we tell the dying person, "Depart, O Christian soul, out of this world" (BCP 464). It is time to leave on your journey.

Just as we pray for travelers in this world, we pray for the dying who prepare to set forth and for the dead who travel to the other side. We also pray for the dead in their new experience, as they continue to grow closer to God and to experience the light of Christ.

Those who are dying
Those who rest in Christ and all the dead

Father of all, we pray to you for N., and for all those whom we love but see no longer. Grant to them eternal rest. Let light perpetual shine upon them. May *his/her* soul and the souls of all the departed, through the mercy of God, rest in peace.

BCP, Burial II

Those whose death is unknown or unmourned
Those seeking Christ beyond the grave
Every Christian soul

> God of mercy, accept the prayers we offer you this day. Increase, we pray, our faith, deepen our hope, and confirm us in your eternal love. We ask this in the name of Jesus Christ our Lord.
>
> *BAS, Funeral I, adapted*

The dead on their anniversaries

> For Christ is risen from the dead, trampling down death by death and giving life to those in the tomb, and we give you glory, Father, Son, and Holy Spirit, for ever and ever.

9

Ancient Litanies

L itanies of intercession used by early Christians show how the people of God interpreted the needs of society in their own time. Some of these concerns remain significant. Others are no longer important, and when we pray we replace them with concerns of our own age.

The following litanies are taken from liturgical texts in the *Apostolic Constitutions*, a document written in Syria in the late fourth century and based on earlier sources. They include five litanies at the eucharist as well as litanies at evening prayer, morning prayer, and funerals. These are the earliest complete intercessions that have survived from the ancient church.[1]

A. Prayers at the Eucharist

After the bishop's teaching or homily, all stand and the deacon ascends the *bema* (a high place for the readings and prayers) and calls out: "None of the hearers [remain]! None of the unbelievers [remain]!" In succession the deacon bids prayers for catechumens, energumens, illuminands, and penitents, and dismisses each category. The deacon then leads the faithful in the general intercessions of the faithful. In each of the five litanies the people respond *Kyrie eleison* after each bidding or petition, and the bishop ends with a blessing or prayer.

---

1 The text is translated from the Greek and Latin in F. X. Funk, ed., *Didascalia et Constitutiones Apostolorum* (Paderborn: Schoenig, 1905). See also W. Jardine Grisbrooke, ed., *The Liturgical Portions of the Apostolic Constitutions*, Alcuin/GROW Liturgical Study 13-14 (Bramcote, Notts.: Grove Books Ltd., 1990).

Litany for the Catechumens

For the catechumens let us call earnestly on God, that he who is good and the lover of humanity will favorably listen to their prayers and supplications and, receiving their petitions, will help them and grant them the requests of their hearts for their good.

That he may reveal to them the gospel of his Christ.

That he may enlighten and educate them.

That he may instruct them in the knowledge of God.

That he may teach them his commandments and judgments.

That he may plant in them his pure and saving fear.

That he may open the ears of their hearts to apply themselves to his law day and night.

That he may establish them in godliness.

That he may unite and number them with his holy flock, counting them worthy of the washing of rebirth, of the garment of incorruption, of the true life.

That he may deliver them from all ungodliness and give no place to the adversary against them.

That he may cleanse them from all dirt of flesh and spirit, and may dwell in them, and walk [in them] through his Christ.

That he may bless their comings and their goings and order their affairs for good.

Again let us earnestly make our supplications for them, that obtaining remission of sins by initiation they may be made worthy of the holy mysteries and of communion with the saints.

Catechumens, rise.

Ask for the peace of God through his Christ.

That this day and all the time of your life may be peaceful and without sin.

That your end may be Christian.

That God may be merciful and benevolent.

For the forgiveness of your sins.

Commend yourselves to the one and unbegotten God through his Christ.

Bow down and receive the blessing.

The bishop blesses the catechumens with a long prayer, and the deacon says, "Catechumens, go in peace."

Litany for the Energumens

> Pray, you who are possessed by unclean spirits.
> Let us all earnestly pray for them.
>> That God, the lover of humanity, may through Christ rebuke the unclean and evil spirits and rescue his supplicants from the tyranny of the adversary.
>> That he who rebuked the legion of demons and the devil, the prince of wickedness, may now rebuke the apostates from ungodliness, and rescue his own handiwork from their activity, and purify those whom he made with such great wisdom.
>
> Again let us earnestly pray for them.
> Save them and raise them up, O God, in your power.

The bishop prays at length to Christ to rebuke the evil spirits, and the deacon says, "You who are possessed, go."

Litany for the Illuminands

> Pray, you who are to be enlightened.
> All we the faithful, let us earnestly pray for them.
>> That when they have been initiated into the death of Christ, the Lord will count them worthy to rise with him and to become sharers in his kingdom and partakers of his mysteries.
>> That he may unite and number them with the saved in his holy church.
>
> Again let us earnestly pray for them.
> Save them and raise them up in your grace.
>
> Bow down, you who have been signed to God through his Christ.

The bishop blesses the illuminands (those in the last stages of preparation for baptism), and the deacon says, "You who are to be enlightened, go."

Litany for the Penitents

Pray, you who are penitents.

Let us all earnestly pray for our penitent brothers [and sisters].

That the loving and merciful God may show them the way of repentance.

That he will accept their return and confession.

And quickly beat down Satan under their feet.

And deliver them from the snare of the devil and from the intrigues of demons.

And keep them from every unlawful word, and from every unseemly deed, and from wicked thought.

And blot out the handwriting against them, and write them in the book of life.

And purify them from every filth of flesh and spirit and, having restored them, unite them to his holy flock.

For he knows whereof we are made—for who can boast that he is pure of heart, or who can truly say that he is clean from sin?—for we all are among the punishable.

Again let us earnestly pray for them, for there is joy in heaven over one sinner who repents.

That turning from every unlawful work they may devote themselves to every good deed.

So that God, the lover of humanity, speedily and favorably accepting their prayers, may restore them to their former dignity, give them the joy of salvation, and strengthen them with his guiding Spirit.

That their steps may no longer slip, but that they may be counted worthy to be partakers of his holy gifts and sharers in the divine mysteries.

That being shown worthy of adoption, they may obtain eternal life.

Again let us earnestly say for them: Lord, have mercy.

Save them, O God, and raise them up by your mercy.

Rising, bow down before God through his Christ and receive the blessing.

The bishop blesses them, asking for restoration to the holy church, and the deacon says, "Penitents, go."

Litany of the Faithful

Let no unauthorized person draw near. All we the faithful, let us bend the knee, let us pray to God through his Christ, let us all earnestly call upon God through his Christ.

For the peace and tranquility of the world and of the holy churches let us pray, that the God of the universe grant us his perpetual and stable peace, and keep us persevering in the fullness of virtue and godliness.

For the holy catholic and apostolic church from one end of the earth to another let us pray, that the Lord continually guard and preserve it until the end of the world, unshaken by waves and storms, and founded on the rock.

And for the holy parish [i.e., diocese] in this place let us pray, that the Lord of the universe make us worthy without turning back to press after the hope of heaven, and without ceasing to pay him the debt of our prayer.

For every bishop under heaven, who rightly determines the word of your truth, let us pray.

And for our bishop James and his parishes, for our bishop Clement and his parishes, for our bishop Evodius and his parishes, for our bishop Annianus and his parishes,[2] let us pray, that the God of mercy preserve them for the good of the holy churches, in safety, honor, and length of days, and give them an honorable old age in piety and justice.

And for our presbyters let us pray, that the Lord deliver them from every unseemly and evil deed and grant them a secure and honorable presbyterate.

For all the deacons and ministers in Christ let us pray, that the Lord grant them a blameless ministry.

For the readers, singers, virgins, widows, and orphans let us pray, for married women and women in childbirth let us pray, that the Lord have mercy on them all.

For eunuchs [i.e., ascetics] who walk in holy paths let us pray, for those who live in continence and godliness let us pray.

For those who bear the fruit of good works in the holy church and give alms to the needy let us pray, for those who bring offerings and

---

2   Those named in this bidding are the ancient bishops of Jerusalem, Rome, Antioch, and Alexandria and their parishes [dioceses].

firstfruits to the Lord our God let us pray, that the God of all goodness repay them with heavenly gifts, and give them in this world hundredfold, and in the world to come life eternal, and bestow on them for temporal goods eternal ones, and for earthly goods heavenly ones.

For our brothers [and sisters] newly enlightened, let us pray, that the Lord strengthen and confirm them.

For our brothers [and sisters] afflicted by illness let us pray, that the Lord deliver them from all sickness and all infirmity and restore them in health to his holy church.

For those who travel by water and land let us pray, for those in the mines, in exile, in prison, and in bonds for the name of the Lord let us pray, for those oppressed in bitter servitude let us pray.

For our enemies and those who hate us let us pray, for those who persecute us because of the name of the Lord let us pray, that the Lord calm their anger and scatter their wrath against us.

For those who are outside [the church] and wandering in error let us pray, that the Lord convert them.

Let us keep in mind the children of the church, that the Lord perfect them in his fear and grant them length of days.

For one another let us pray, that the Lord by his grace keep us and guard us to the end, deliver us from the evil one and from all the scandals of those who work iniquity, and bring us in safety to his heavenly kingdom.

For every Christian soul let us pray.

Save us and raise us up, O God, by your mercy.

Let us rise. Praying earnestly, let us commend ourselves and one another to the living God through his Christ.

The bishop prays at length, asking God to look down "on this your flock," to purify them, sanctify them, protect them, deliver them from every evil, and grant them eternal life. The deacon says, "Let us attend," and the liturgy continues with the kiss of peace.

B. Prayers at the Daily Office

The daily office of the fourth century has similar biddings, expanded to include topics of the evening or morning. As listed in the *Apostolic Constitutions*, the biddings only indicate topics. The actual biddings were probably more extensive, and the response is assumed.

In the evening office the deacon first bids prayers for catechumens, energumens, illuminands, and penitents, and dismisses them. Then the deacon begins:

All we the faithful, let us pray to the Lord.

The deacon then sings an extensive litany like the one in the eucharist. The litany concludes:

Save us and raise us up, O God, by your Christ.

Standing up, let us ask for the mercies of the Lord and his compassions.
    For the angel of peace.
    For things that are good and profitable.
    For a Christian end.
    For an evening and a night of peace, free from sin.

Let us ask that the whole of our life be without reproach.

Let us commend ourselves and one another to the living God through his Christ.

The litany in the morning office is similar, ending:

Save us, O God, and raise us up by your grace.

Let us ask of the Lord, of his mercies and compassions, that this morning and day be peaceful and without sin, and also all the time of our journey.
    For the angel of peace.
    For a Christian end.
    That God be merciful and gracious.

Let us commend ourselves and one another to the living God though his only begotten.

C. Prayers at a Funeral

The deacon's litany at a funeral is similar to the ones in the eucharist and daily office. After the usual biddings for the church and the world, the deacon concludes:

> Let us pray also for our brothers [and sisters] who are at rest in Christ.
> For the repose of this man [woman].

> Let us pray that God, the lover of humanity, may receive his [her] soul, forgive him [her] every sin, voluntary and involuntary, and be merciful and gracious to him [her], and give him [her] his [her] lot in the land of the righteous who rest in the bosom of Abraham and Isaac and Jacob, with all who have pleased him and done his will from the beginning of the world, from where sorrow, sadness, and sighing have fled away.

> Let us rise. Let us commend ourselves and one another to the eternal God through the Word in the beginning.

10

Sample Litanies

L ike the forms for intercessory prayer provided in the *Book of Common Prayer*, the litanies of intercession in this chapter are only examples. They show how a community can compose intercessions, based on ancient and modern models. Instead of using them as printed here, congregations should adapt and change them for their own circumstances, or compose entirely new forms based on these models.

A. Prayers at Morning and Evening

Morning

Deacon or other leader
Let us complete our morning sacrifice.

The people may offer their own names and concerns or pray freely.

For a day that is holy, good, and peaceful.
Kyrie eleison [or similar response].
For an angel of peace to guide us in all our paths.
For [this holy gathering and for] the people of God in every place.
For all nations, peoples, tribes, clans, and families.
For all that is good and bountiful in the world.
For all those in danger and need: the sick and the suffering, prisoners, captives, and their families, the hungry, homeless, and oppressed.

For the dying and the dead.

For our deliverance from all affliction, strife, and need.

Lifting our voices with all creation, with earth and water, fire and air, all things living and all things dead, [with...], let us commend ourselves and one another to the living God through Christ.
To you, O Lord.

Presider

Eternal God, whose light divides the day from the night and turns the shadow of death into the morning, drive far from us all wrong desires, incline our hearts to keep your law, and guide our feet into the way of peace, that, having done your will with cheerfulness during the day, we may, when night comes, rejoice to give you thanks; through Jesus Christ our Lord. *Amen.*

Evening

Deacon or other leader

Let us complete our evening sacrifice.

The people may offer their own names and concerns or pray freely.

For an evening [and night] that is holy, good, and peaceful.
Kyrie eleison [or similar response].

For an angel of peace to guide us in all our paths.

For peace in the holy church and in the whole world.

For the pardon and forgiveness of our sins and offenses.

For all that is good and bountiful to our souls.

For a Christian end to our lives and for all who have fallen asleep in Christ.

Remembering our most glorious and blessed Virgin Mary and all the saints, let us commend ourselves and one another to the living God through Christ.
To you, O Lord.

Presider

Blessed are you, O Lord, the God of our ancestors, creator of the changes of day and night, giving rest to the weary, renewing the strength of those who are spent, bestowing upon us occasions of song in the evening. As you have protected us in the day that is past, so be with us in the coming night. Keep us from every sin, every evil, and every fear, for you are our light and salvation, and the strength of our life. To you be glory for endless ages. *Amen.*

B. Prayers at the Eucharist

A Litany for Rite One
This litany is based on the traditional prayer "for the whole state of Christ's Church and the world," which dates from the 1549 prayer book. Instead of addressing petitions to God, however, the leader bids the people pray for certain names and concerns. Most of the biddings are adapted from the 1979 prayer book; the final bidding, in praise of the blessed Virgin Mary and all the saints, is based on the 1549 book.

Deacon or other leader
Let us pray for the whole state of Christ's church and the world.

The people may offer their own names and concerns or pray freely. After each of the following petitions the people may make a response such as, "Lord, give thy heavenly grace" or "Lord, hear our prayer."

Let us offer prayers unto the divine majesty, beseeching God to inspire continually the universal church with the spirit of truth, unity, and concord, that all those who confess the holy name may agree in the truth of God's holy word, and live in unity and godly love.

For *N.* our bishop, and for all bishops, priests, deacons, and other ministers, that they may, both by their life and doctrine, set forth the true and lively word of God, and rightly and duly administer his holy sacraments.

For all people, and especially this congregation, that, with meek heart and due reverence, they may hear and receive God's holy word, truly serving him in holiness and righteousness all the days of their life.

For those who bear the authority of government in this and every land [especially *N.N.*], that God may rule their hearts and lead them to wise decisions and right actions for the welfare and peace of the world.

For all that is good and bountiful in the world, that all people may behold the gracious hand of God in all his works and, rejoicing in his whole creation, honor him with their substance and be faithful stewards of his bounty.

For all those who, in this transitory life, are in trouble, sorrow, need, sickness, or any other adversity, that God may comfort and succor them.

For all those departed this life in the faith and fear of God [especially *N.N.*], beseeching him to grant them continual growth in his love and service.

Let us give unto God most high praise and hearty thanks for the wonderful grace and virtue declared in all his saints from the beginning of the world, and chiefly in the glorious and most blessed Virgin Mary, mother of Jesus Christ our Lord and God, and in the holy patriarchs, prophets, apostles, and martyrs, whose examples, steadfastness in faith, and keeping of the holy commandments may the Lord grant us to follow.

Presider

Grant these our prayers, O Father, for Jesus Christ's sake, our only mediator and advocate. *Amen.*

A Litany Based on Ancient Sources

Like Form I in the *Book of Common Prayer* and Litany 1 in the *Book of Alternative Services*, this litany is based on the Great *Ektene*, which occurs near the beginning of the Divine Liturgy in Eastern Orthodox churches, with the addition of a bidding for the dead. Its ancient ancestors include the prayers of the faithful in the *Apostolic Constitutions*. This litany is especially appropriate for Sundays and feasts. If the litany is sung to a tone with a final inflection, the phrase "let us pray to the Lord" may be omitted.

Presider or deacon

Let us pray to God through Christ and earnestly call upon God to hear our prayers. *[The invitation may also reflect the day, season, or occasion.]*

The people may offer their own names and concerns or pray freely. After each of the following petitions the people sing, "Kyrie eleison" or "Lord, have mercy."

Deacon or other leader

In peace let us pray to the Lord.

For peace from on high and for our salvation, let us pray to the Lord.

For the peace of the whole world, for the welfare of the holy churches of God, and for the unity of all, let us pray to the Lord.

For this holy gathering and for those who enter with faith, reverence, and fear of God, let us pray to the Lord.

For *N.* our bishop and all bishops, for the presbyters, for the deacons and all who minister in Christ, and for all the holy people of God, let us pray to the Lord.

For the leaders of our country, for all in civil authority, and for those who guard the peace, let us pray to the Lord.

For this city [village, place], for every city and place, and for those who live in them, let us pray to the Lord.

For good weather, for abundant fruits of the earth, and for peaceful times, let us pray to the Lord.

For travelers by land, by water, and by air, for the sick and the suffering, for prisoners, the oppressed, and all those in danger and need, and for their salvation, let us pray to the Lord.

For our brothers and sisters who rest in Christ and for all the dead, let us pray to the Lord.

For our deliverance from all affliction, strife, and need, let us pray to the Lord.

Remembering the blessed Virgin Mary and all the saints, let us commend ourselves and one another to the living God through Christ.
To you, O Lord.

Presider

Almighty God, who has given us grace at this time with one accord to make our common supplications to you, and who has promised through your well-beloved Son that when two or three are gathered in his name you will hear their requests, fulfill now our desires and petitions as may be best for us, granting us in this world knowledge of your truth, and in the age to come eternal life; for you, O Father, are good and loving, and we glorify you through your Son Jesus Christ our Lord, in the Holy Spirit, now and for ever. *Amen.*

A Litany for Weekdays

Those who lead intercessions for weekday liturgies often have to compose them spontaneously. At these times it helps to reduce the litany to four easily remembered categories—church, world, needy, and community—and perhaps to add a commemoration of the saints, as in this example.

Presider or deacon
> Let us earnestly call upon God to hear our prayers.

The people may offer their own names and concerns or pray freely. After each of the following petitions the people sing, "Kyrie eleison" or "Lord, have mercy."

Deacon or other leader
> For the holy church of God, filled by the Spirit, that all may be one in Christ, let us pray to the Lord.
>
> For the world and its people, that all may live in justice and freedom, peace and godliness, let us pray to the Lord.
>
> For those in need, the suffering and the oppressed, travelers and prisoners, the dying and the dead, that all may live in safety and the hope of eternal life, let us pray to the Lord.
>
> For ourselves and our congregation, that we may glorify God and share in the heavenly kingdom, let us pray to the Lord.
>
> Remembering the blessed Virgin Mary and all the saints, let us commend ourselves and one another to the living God through Christ.
> *To you, O Lord.*

Presider
> O Lord our God, hear the fervent prayers of your people. In the multitude of your mercies, look with compassion on us and all who turn to you for help. For you are gracious, O lover of souls, and we give you glory, Father, Son, and Holy Spirit, now and for ever. *Amen.*

C. Prayers at Seasonal Liturgies

Advent

Presider or deacon
> As we prepare to meet the Lord Jesus, let us offer prayers to God who comes as the rising sun into the darkness of our lives.

The people may offer their own names and concerns or pray freely. After each of the following petitions the people sing, "Come, O Lord, and save us" or a similar response.

Deacon or other leader

For the coming of Jesus Christ in power and glory, let us pray to the Lord.

For the coming of Wisdom to teach and guide us, let us pray to the Lord.

For the coming of Emmanuel, the hope of all the peoples, let us pray to the Lord.

For the peace of the world, and for our unity in Christ, let us pray to the Lord.

For N. our bishop and all bishops, for the presbyters, for the deacons and all who minister in Christ, and for all the holy people of God, let us pray to the Lord.

For the church throughout the world and the faithful in every place, let us pray to the Lord.

For the leaders of the nations and all in authority, let us pray to the Lord.

For justice, peace, and freedom among peoples of the earth, let us pray to the Lord.

For travelers, for the sick and the suffering, for the hungry and oppressed, and for those in prison, let us pray to the Lord.

For the dying and the dead, let us pray to the Lord.

For our deliverance from all affliction, strife, and need, let us pray to the Lord.

Joining our voices with the blessed Virgin Mary and with all the saints and angels of God, let us commend ourselves and one another to the living God through Christ.

To you, O Lord.

For the concluding collect, the following prayers may be used on the traditional days of the O Antiphons, as indicated, and on any other day in Advent.

December 17

O Wisdom, breath from the mouth of God most high, who reigns from one end of the earth to the other, and governs all creation with strong and tender care, come and teach us the way of wisdom. Glory to you for ever. *Amen.*

December 18

O Adonai, Lord of the house of Israel, who appeared to Moses in a burning bush and gave him the law on Sinai, come and stretch out your hand to set us free. Glory to you for ever. *Amen.*

December 19

O Root of Jesse, who rises as a signal among all peoples, in whose presence rulers stand silent and nations bow in worship, come and deliver us without delay. Glory to you for ever. *Amen.*

December 20

O Key of David, scepter of the house of Israel, you open and none can shut, you shut and none can open. Come and free the captives from prison, who sit in darkness and the shadow of death. Glory to you for ever. *Amen.*

December 21

O Rising Sun, brightness of light eternal, sun of justice, come and shine on those who sit in darkness and the shadow of death. Glory to you for ever. *Amen.*

December 22

O King of all the nations, only joy of every heart, keystone of the mighty arch who makes us one, come and save the creature you fashioned from clay. Glory to you for ever. *Amen.*

December 23

O Emmanuel, our king and lawgiver, desire of all nations and Savior of all peoples, come and save us, O Lord our God. Glory to you for ever. *Amen.*

Christmas, Epiphany, and Baptism

Presider or deacon

As we join the whole creation and celebrate with joy the Word made flesh, let us offer prayers to God who dwells among us to the end of time.

The people may offer their own names and concerns or pray freely. After each of the following petitions the people sing, "Lord, grant us peace," "Hear our prayer, Lord of glory!" or a similar response.

Deacon or other leader

> *[Christmas]* By the birth of the timeless Son of God in the womb of the Virgin Mary, let us pray to the Lord.
>
> *[Christmas]* By the wedding of the human and divine natures in Christ Jesus, let us pray to the Lord.
>
> *[Epiphany]* By the manifestation of the King of the Jews to the shepherds and the magi, let us pray to the Lord.
>
> *[Baptism of Christ]* By the baptism of the Son of God in the river Jordan, let us pray to the Lord.
>
> *[Miracle at Cana]* By the water made wine at Cana of Galilee, let us pray to the Lord.
>
> For *N.* our bishop and the presbyters, for the deacons and all who minister in Christ, and for all the holy people of God, let us pray to the Lord.
>
> For all believers who put their trust in the incarnate Son of God, let us pray to the Lord.
>
> For the leaders of the nations and all in authority, and for peace and justice, let us pray to the Lord.
>
> For the conversion of the whole human race to our blessed Lord and Savior Jesus Christ, let us pray to the Lord.
>
> For travelers, for the sick and the suffering, for the hungry and oppressed, for those in prison, and for the dying and the dead, let us pray to the Lord.
>
> Remembering our most glorious and blessed Virgin Mary and all the saints, let us commend ourselves and one another to the living God through Christ.
>
> *To you, O Lord.*

Presider

> Source of light and gladness, accept the prayers we offer on this joyful feast. May we grow up in Jesus Christ who unites our lives to yours and who is Lord for all eternity. For you created all things and gave them life through the Word, and we give you glory, Father, Son, and Holy Spirit, for ever and ever. *Amen.*

Lent (Sundays 1-3)

On the first Sunday in Lent, if the assembly is enrolling catechumens as candidates for baptism, a special litany is used (BOS 122).

Presider or deacon
> In this holy fast of Lent, let us offer prayers to God who leads us through the wilderness and gives us water to drink.

The people may offer their own names and concerns or pray freely. After each of the following petitions the people sing, "Kyrie eleison," "Lord, have mercy," or a similar response.

Deacon or other leader
> For peace from on high and for our salvation, let us pray to the Lord.
> For the peace of the whole world, for the welfare of the holy churches of God, and for the unity of all, let us pray to the Lord.
> For N. our bishop and the presbyters, for the deacons and all who minister in Christ, and for all the holy people of God, let us pray to the Lord.
> For the catechumens who have received the sign of the cross, and for their teachers and sponsors, let us pray to the Lord.
> For all who await with expectation the grace of the Holy Spirit, let us pray to the Lord.
> For those who bow their knees and hearts before the God of mercy, let us pray to the Lord.
> For the strengthening gifts of the Holy Spirit to do all that pleases our Father, let us pray to the Lord.
> For the blessed fruits of the Holy Spirit and the crucifixion of all self-indulgence and wicked desires, let us pray to the Lord.
> For the grace to pray, fast, and give alms as the Lord wills, let us pray to the Lord.
> For the destruction of demonic powers and all that lifts itself up against the anointed Son of God, let us pray to the Lord.
> For our deliverance from all affliction, strife, and need, let us pray to the Lord.
> Remembering the blessed Virgin Mary and all the saints, let us commend ourselves and one another to the living God through Christ.
> *To you, O Lord.*

Presider

O Lord our God, mercifully hear the prayers of all who thirst and turn to you, for you chose your people to be born of water and the Spirit, and we give you glory, O Father, with your Son through the Holy Spirit, now and for ever. *Amen.*

Lent (Sundays 4–6)

Presider or deacon

In this holy season of Lent, as we prepare for the feast of the resurrection, let us offer prayers to God who opens the graves of the dead.

The people may offer their own names and concerns or pray freely. After each of the following petitions the people sing, "Kyrie eleison," "Lord, have mercy," or a similar response.

Among the special intentions, a leader names the candidates for baptism and their sponsors.

Deacon or other leader

For the unity, peace, and welfare of the church of Christ, let us pray to the Lord.

For new brothers and sisters in the faith and unity of the one, holy, catholic, and apostolic church, let us pray to the Lord.

For the catechumens who await the illumination of Christ, and for their teachers and sponsors, let us pray to the Lord.

For preachers of the gospel who speak the truth in love, let us pray to the Lord.

For prophets fired by God's word and for theologians who seek God alone, let us pray to the Lord.

For all who serve the needs and defend the rights of men and women, let us pray to the Lord.

For the elimination of slavery, exploitation, and war, let us pray to the Lord.

For the gifts of nature and of grace we need to live full lives and serve the gospel, let us pray to the Lord.

For the sick and the handicapped, prisoners and those on death row, and for all the faithful departed, let us pray to the Lord.

Remembering the blessed Virgin Mary and all the saints, let us commend ourselves and one another to the living God through Christ.
To you, O Lord.

Presider

God of justice and mercy, hear the petitions of your faithful people and grant us a place at your table in heaven. For you give us resurrection and life in Christ the Son of God, and we give you glory, O Father, with your Son through the Holy Spirit, now and for ever. *Amen.*

The Great Vigil of Easter

Presider or deacon

Joined by those who are newly baptized in Christ, and filled with joy on this queen of feasts, let us offer prayers to God who fills the darkness of the world with the light of Christ.

The people may offer their own names and concerns or pray freely. After each of the following petitions the people sing, "Hear our prayer, Lord of glory!" or a similar response.

Among the special intentions, a leader names the newly baptized and their sponsors.

Deacon or other leader

In peace let us pray to the Lord.

For the holy churches of God, for N. our bishop, for the presbyters and deacons, and for all the holy people of God, that our Savior may grant us triumph over our visible and invisible enemies, let us pray to the Lord.

For the world and its leaders, our nation and its people, that with Christ we may crush beneath our feet the prince of darkness and all his evil powers, let us pray to the Lord.

For all those in need, the suffering and the oppressed, travelers and prisoners, the dying and the dead, that Christ may fill them with the joy and happiness of his holy resurrection, let us pray to the Lord.

For ourselves and our communities of faith, that we may enter the chamber of the divine wedding feast and rejoice without limit with the angels and saints in the church at rest, let us pray to the Lord.

Remembering our most glorious and blessed Virgin Mary and all the saints, let us commend ourselves and one another to the living God through Christ.

To you, O Lord.

Presider

Blessed are you, O Lord our God, who destroyed death and brought life and immortality to light. Hear our prayers which we offer in the hope of eternal glory. For Christ is risen from the dead, trampling down death by death and giving life to those in the tomb, and we give you glory, Father, Son, and Holy Spirit, now and always and unto the ages of ages. *Amen.*

The Fifty Days of Easter

Presider or deacon

Filled with joy in these fifty days of Easter, let us offer prayers to God who raised Christ from the dead and sent the Spirit to dwell among us.

The people may offer their own names and concerns or pray freely. After each of the following petitions the people sing, "Hear our prayer, Lord of glory!" or a similar response.

Deacon or other leader

In peace let us pray to the Lord.

For peace from on high and for our salvation, let us pray to the Lord.

For the peace of the whole world, for the welfare of the holy churches of God, and for the unity of all, let us pray to the Lord.

For this holy gathering and for those who enter with faith, reverence, and fear of God, let us pray to the Lord.

For our new brothers and sisters illumined by the light of Christ, let us pray to the Lord.

For N. our bishop and the presbyters, for the deacons and all who minister in Christ, and for all the holy people of God, let us pray to the Lord.

For the world and its leaders, our nation and its people, let us pray to the Lord.

For all those in need, the suffering and the oppressed, travelers and prisoners, the dying and the dead, let us pray to the Lord.

For ourselves and our communities of faith, let us pray to the Lord.

That the Lord Jesus Christ our Savior may grant us triumph over the temptations of our visible and invisible enemies, let us pray to the Lord.

That we may crush beneath our feet the prince of darkness and all his evil powers, let us pray to the Lord.

That Christ may raise us up with him and make us rise from the tomb of our sins and offenses, let us pray to the Lord.

That he may fill us with the joy and happiness of his holy resurrection, let us pray to the Lord.

That we may enter the chamber of his divine wedding feast, let us pray to the Lord.

That we may rejoice without limit with angels and saints in the church at rest, let us pray to the Lord.

Remembering our most glorious and blessed Virgin Mary and all the saints, let us commend ourselves and one another to the living God through Christ.

To you, O Lord.

Presider

O Lord our God, receive the prayers we offer this day, and grant that we who have received new life in baptism may live for ever in the joy of the resurrection, through Jesus Christ our Lord. *Amen.*

D. Prayers on Special Occasions

Feasts of Saints

Presider or deacon

On this feast of [All Saints, *N.*], as we recall the blessed ones who have gone before us, let us offer prayers to God who adorns the poor with victory.

The people may offer their own names and concerns or pray freely. After each of the following petitions the people sing, "Kyrie eleison," "Lord, have mercy," or a similar response.

Deacon or other leader

With the angels and archangels and the spirits of the blessed, let us pray to the Lord.

With the Virgin Mary, mother of our Savior, let us pray to the Lord.

With the holy patriarchs, prophets, apostles, and martyrs, let us pray
to the Lord.

With *N.* and all the saints, witnesses to the gospel, let us pray to the Lord.

For *N.* our bishop and the presbyters, for the deacons and all who minister
in Christ, and for all the holy people of God, let us pray to the Lord.

For the church throughout the world and the faithful in every place, let
us pray to the Lord.

For the leaders of the nations and all in authority, let us pray to the Lord.

For travelers, for the sick and the suffering, for those in prison, and for
the dying and the dead, let us pray to the Lord.

For the forgiveness of our sins and offenses, let us pray to the Lord.

For our deliverance from all affliction, strife, and need, let us pray to the
Lord.

Remembering our most glorious and blessed Virgin Mary and all the
saints, let us commend ourselves and one another to the living God
through Christ.

To you, O Lord.

Presider

Blessed are you, O Lord our God, for the triumph of Christ in the lives
of all your saints. Receive the prayers we offer you this day and help us
to run our course with faith, that we may come to your eternal kingdom,
through Jesus Christ our Lord. *Amen.*

Marriage

Presider or deacon

Let us offer to God our petitions for our common humanity, and
especially let us pray for this man and this woman whom God makes
one flesh in holy matrimony.

*The people may offer their own names and concerns or pray freely. After each of
the following petitions the people sing, "Kyrie eleison," "Lord, have mercy," or a
similar response.*

Deacon or other leader

For this holy gathering and for the people of God in every place.

For all nations and peoples.

For all those in danger and need, for those united in marriage, and for all families.

For *N.* and *N.*, that they may taste the wine at the wedding feast and discern the love of Christ.

That they may grow in love and peace with God and one another all their days.

That they may be to each other a strength in need, a counselor in perplexity, a comfort in sorrow, and a companion in joy.

For *[their children,]* their families, and their friends.

For ourselves, that we may find our lives strengthened and our loyalties confirmed.

For our ancestors and all who have gone before us and now rest in peace.

Lifting our voices with all creation, let us commend ourselves and one another to the living God through Christ.

To you, O Lord.

Presider

Blessed are you, O Lord our God, who unites all persons in holy community, and the living to the dead, and especially your servants *N.* and *N.* in marriage. Hear our fervent prayers and transform them and all of us by your grace, that your will may be done on earth as it is in heaven. Glory to you for ever and ever. *Amen.*

Burial of the Dead

Presider or deacon

Let us offer to God our petitions for the living and the dead, and especially let us pray for those among us who have passed to the other side.

The people may offer their own names and concerns or pray freely. After each of the following petitions the people sing, "Kyrie eleison," "Lord, have mercy," or a similar response.

Deacon or other leader

For this holy gathering and for the people of God in every place.

For all nations, peoples, tribes, clans, and families.

For all those in danger and need, especially the sick and the suffering, those who are dying, and those who have died in the faith of Christ.

For our *brother [sister] N.*, who was washed in baptism and anointed with the Holy Spirit, that *he [she]* may rejoice with the blessed Virgin Mary and all the saints and angels.

For our *brother [sister] N.*, who was nourished with the body and blood of Christ, that *he [she]* may taste the wine at the wedding feast of heaven.

For ourselves, our families and friends, and especially those who mourn, that we may be filled with the joy and happiness of Christ's holy resurrection.

Lifting our voices with all creation, with those in every realm and state of being, let us commend ourselves and one another to the living God through Christ.

To you, O Lord.

Presider

Blessed are you, God of light eternal. You are worthy at all times to be praised by happy voices, by the living and the dead, and especially by your servant *N.* Hear our fervent prayers and give *him [her]* refuge under the shelter of your wings, where the blessed in Christ have everlasting peace. Glory to you for ever. *Amen.*

11

Music

Intercessory prayer takes place within the music of God's creation, as supplication for the cosmic harmony of all things seen and unseen. The purpose of this section, therefore, is to encourage the musical leaders of the church to adapt old chants for intercession and to compose new ones, and to encourage the people to sing them.

In a litany of intercession the chant has two parts: the leader's bidding or petition and the people's response. Although the examples below contain only the people's response, the leader's part is always assumed. Whenever possible, it is desirable to sing both parts. In this way the leader and all the people become performers in a musical ensemble.

The leader's part, called the *recitative*, consists of several melodic elements. Most of this part is sung on a single note, called the *tenor* or reciting note, and it ends with a melodic formula of one or more notes, called the *final cadence*. Although a typical recitative contains only the tenor and final cadence, experienced singers sometimes add other elements. The singer may begin with an introductory phrase, at a pause insert a cadence, and at a major pause modulate or change the reciting note to another pitch.

The response is a brief melodic formula in one or more harmonic parts. It may range in complexity from a simple melody in one part, consisting of two or three notes, to an ornate melodic structure in four-part harmony. The music should be related to the leader's part, so that the leader and people can sing back and forth in a unified melody. To enable this unity, often the leader's reciting note is the same as the first or main note of the response.

It is sometimes desirable to rehearse the people's part, and there are several ways to do this. At the beginning of the intercessions a deacon, song leader, or cantor may introduce the response by singing it. Thereafter, the chant of each recitative gives the people their starting note. In a variation of this method, a musician may play instrumental phrases to teach the people the tune. In another method, before each response the song leader may use an instrument or a pitch pipe to give the starting note.

During the litany, however, it is usually better to sing without accompaniment or with occasional, soft notes from an instrument. In harmonized responses the people may continue humming the last note during the next bidding; this creates an attractive unity and helps to keep the leader on pitch. If the bidding ends with the word "Lord" and the response begins with "Lord," the people may sing the word together with the leader.

The musical responses provided in this chapter are especially designed for litanies of intercession. Congregations may sing them as written or adapt them in a variety of ways. They may substitute different texts for the seasons of the church year and for various occasions, altering the music to suit the words and the nature of the celebration. They may sing them as simple melodies or as complex harmonies.

As throughout this book, all examples are designed to encourage the composition of local prayers.

Chants from the Past

Early plainchant is still widely used in liturgy, including litany responses. One example, adapted from the Litany of the Saints, appears as a *Kyrie eleison* in the *Hymnal 1982* at S95. The music of the last "Lord, have mercy" comes from the ancient melody for *Te rogamus, audi nos* (We beseech you, hear our prayer). This melody has been used with many litanies and is the standard music for the general intercessions in the 1970 Latin edition of *Missale Romanum*. A related melody is "Lord, hear our prayer," the response in the litany for the candidates in Holy Baptism (Hymnal S75).

Several chants in the hymnal come from the middle ages. The *Kyrie* at S84 is the opening chant of *Missa orbis factor*, Mass 11 in *Graduale Romanum*. It may be adapted for intercessory responses, perhaps by using just the first *Kyrie eleison*. A version based on the opening musical phrase of the *Kyrie* appears in the Canadian *Book of Alternative Services* (page 915).

A popular modern chant for "Lord, have mercy" is a harmonized response related to Slavonic tones, with striking similarities to Kievan chant. One of several chants for the prayers of the people in the Episcopal Church and the Anglican Church of Canada, it is used mainly when the litany follows the style of Eastern Orthodox models. One version appears at Hymnal S106 (for Form I) and another at BAS 915. The example below is a simplified version of this chant:

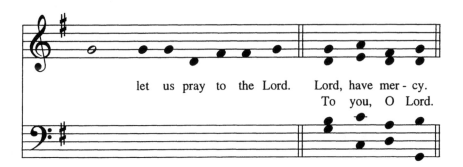

Kievan Chant

The singing of Russian and other Slavonic churches of Eastern Europe has a history parallel to that of western music. One of its early chants, known as *znamenny*, appeared in the twelfth century and went through several phases of development centered in Moscow over the following few centuries. Like western plainchant, *znamenny* is an elevated form of monophonic speech.

Kievan chant is a late variant of *znamenny* chant, consisting of beautiful yet simple melodies adorned with harmony. This chant originated with monks in the ancient cultural center of Kiev and is still sung in Russian and Ukrainian churches. For this and other polyphonic music, the congregation, or at least the choir, should be encouraged to sing in parts; it helps if several experienced singers lead them.

The following chants show several other ways of singing the responses to intercessory petitions, and are based on the famous Kievan chant for the litany at the beginning of the Divine Liturgy. For Advent, Christmas, Lent, and Easter, the examples use a seasonal response. In Kievan chant, as in many other Slavonic chants, there are several different melodies for the "Lord, have mercy" response, used alternatively after different biddings. The example below provides three of these melodies.

The music of the final response, "To you, O Lord," is similar to that of the third "Lord, have mercy." Usually a congregation sings the melodies in rotation—the first one after the first bidding, the second after the second, the third after the third, and starting over on the fourth bidding. The people may start by learning just one melody, probably the first; as they become familiar with it, they may add the other two. For variety they may sing a different melody during a different season—for example, alternating the three melodies during ordinary time in winter, summer, and autumn.

The leader sings the biddings on F with an ending inflection. The chant need not be limited to one note, however. In Eastern Orthodoxy many deacons sing a more complicated melody, ranging up and down from the reciting note.[1]

---

1 Other litany responses of the Eastern Orthodox churches are available in various publications. A large collection of litany chants, with the text in English, appears in *The Divine Liturgy* (Crestwood, N.Y.: St. Vladimir's Seminary Press, 1982).

Advent

This chant uses the first melody of the Kievan chant with the Advent response "Come, O Lord, and save us." It shows how composers can adapt litany music to different seasons and occasions. The leader sings the tenor on F.

Christmas

Similarly, this response for a Christmas litany uses the third melody of the Kievan chant with "Lord, grant us peace." The leader sings the tenor on F.

Lent

For Lent, a simplified version of the first Kievan melody may be used, with the response "Lord, have mercy." The tenor is F, and the people should sing their response slowly.

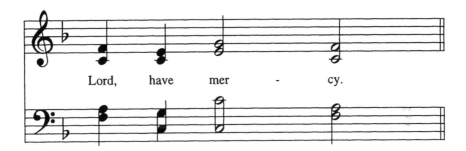

Easter

This Easter chant (which also may be used at Christmas) uses the second melody of the Kievan chant with "Hear our prayer, Lord of glory." The leader sings the tenor on F. The chant may also be used at Christmas.

A Guide for Study and Practice

If congregations want to bring freshness and vitality to their intercessory prayer, they will find it useful to study the topic in small groups. Those who are appointed to lead the prayers on Sunday—deacons, readers, lay eucharistic ministers, and others—may find it helpful to study the topic together. The same groups can also practice writing and leading the prayers of the people.

The following questions and suggestions for discussion, grouped according to chapter, may help in designing group sessions. Encourage the participants to read the chapter before coming to the meeting for discussion.

Theological Background

Chapter 1: A Song of Remembering

1. Does God hear our prayers? Does God act on our requests? Does God care about human beings and all creation?

2. Discuss these types of prayer: praise, thanksgiving, confession, petition, intercession. Which types do you associate with specific parts of the eucharistic liturgy?

3. How is intercession an act of sacrifice?

4. What does intercession have to do with the kingdom of God?

5. How does intercession involve thanksgiving?

6. Why is intercession a song of remembering?

Chapter 2: A Song of Speaking
1. What is the earliest incident of intercession recorded in the Bible? What is the style of this discourse?

2. Discuss other references to intercession in the Hebrew scriptures.

3. What style of prayer does Jesus use?

4. How do authors of the Christian scriptures treat prayer for rulers and other political authorities?

Chapter 3: A Song of Offering
1. In the early church, intercession was the first public act of a newly baptized Christian. Discuss the theological significance of the connection between baptism and intercession.

2. In the early church, where did intercessory prayers occur in the eucharistic liturgy? Why?

3. In the Syrian church of the fourth century, what where the four classes of persons prayed for (and dismissed) before the prayers of the faithful? Do we still have any of these classes? What do we call them today?

4. Discuss the controversy over whether Christians address intercession to the first person or the second person of the Trinity.

5. Why did public intercession virtually disappear from the liturgy during the middle ages? What were the consequences?

6. How did Cranmer treat intercession in the 1549 and 1552 prayer books? Why?

7. In liturgies of our own age, why have intercessions been restored to their ancient position and prominence?

Chapter 4: Week by Week
1. Do we have to use the forms for intercession printed in the prayer book? Discuss the freedom we have to intercede in the eucharist. What are the restrictions?

2. Discuss the origin, form, style, and content of the intercessory prayer in Rite One (BCP 328-330). Discuss the six printed forms for the prayers of the people in the prayer book (BCP 383-393).

3. Which of the printed forms (if any) does your congregation use? Why?

4. Does your congregation use more than one form? Why? Why not?

Chapter 5: Day by Day
1. Discuss your daily use of intercession.

2. In your daily prayer, how do you decide whom or what to pray for?

3. Do you pray alone or with others? If others are available for prayer, why do you (or don't you) pray with them?

4. Do you use the daily office or another form? Why?

5. Do you pray at the evening meal? If so, do you include intercession? If not, try it during the coming week.

Chapter 6: Season by Season
1. List the images and themes of each season: Advent, Christmas, Epiphany, Lent, and Easter. List some of the images and themes of the Sundays in the season after Pentecost.

2. How can your congregation use these seasonal images and themes in intercessory prayer?

Composing the Prayers

Sunday Intercessions

1. Form a committee of three or four persons from your discussion group to compose the prayers of the people for next Sunday morning. (If the discussion group is small, the entire group may do this task. If the group has more than four participants, the committees may each choose a Sunday to compose the prayers.)

2. Choose the form you will use as a model for the prayers. Why did you choose it?

3. During the week, read newspapers, watch television news programs, and be alert to what is going on. What is happening in the world, the nation, your city or village? What are the concerns of the church community? Any serious problems? Take notes.

4. Choose one person to write the biddings or petitions an hour or so before the eucharist. (For ease of editing, you may find it helpful to use a computer.) Then read them aloud to the group. Suggest and make changes. Write them in final form (or print them out) for use in the eucharist. If there is a standard response, only those leading the intercession will need a copy.

5. Choose the leader of the intercessions. Why did you choose this person?

6. Do this for several weeks. After each liturgy, during the coffee hour, listen and ask around for reactions.

7. Did you change the form each week or use the same form (and responses) throughout the period of trial use? Why?

8. Discuss whether you should make seasonal changes to the intercessions. Why?

9. Try writing the presider's introduction and collect, or ask the presider to do this, perhaps improvising at the last moment.

10. Try composing a form of intercession for the Sunday liturgy that includes *all*

the topics listed in chapter 8. (Hint: You do not have to list every topic by name. Link groups of topics under general headings.)

Intercessions on Special Occasions

1. Compose the prayers of the people for the patronal feast of your congregation. (See chapter 7 for background material and suggestions.)

2. Compose the prayers for the last (or the next) marriage in your church family.

3. Compose the prayers of the people for the last funeral in your congregation.

Litanies

1. One Sunday, use the Litany of the Faithful from the *Apostolic Constitutions* provided in chapter 9 as the prayers of the people in your congregation. You must change some phrases to make them appropriate for your people. Tell the congregation beforehand what they are going to do.

2. One Sunday, use the sample litany for Rite One provided in chapter 10. Tell the people beforehand what they are going to do.

3. Try composing other litanies, as needed, in the same way.

Music

1. If your congregation is not accustomed to singing intercessions, try introducing one of the sung responses provided in chapter 11. Have a cantor lead them by singing an introductory phrase, such as "let us pray to the Lord" or "Lord, in your mercy."

2. During the season of Advent (or any other season), use the suggested melody provided in chapter 11 for a sung response.

COWLEY PUBLICATIONS is a ministry of the brothers of the Society of Saint John the Evangelist, a monastic order in the Episcopal Church. Our mission is to provide books and resources for those seeking spiritual and theological formation. COWLEY PUBLICATIONS is committed to developing a new generation of writers and teachers who will encourage people to think and pray in new ways about spirituality, reconciliation, and the future.